Current Titles

Concepts in the Social Sciences

Discourse

David Howarth

Open University Press
Buckingham · Philadelphia

Open University Press
Celtic Court
22 Ballmoor
Buckingham
MK18 1XW

email: enquiries@openup.co.uk
world wide web: www.openup.co.uk

and
325 Chestnut Street
Philadelphia, PA 19106, USA

First Published 2000

A catalogue record of this book is available from the British Library

ISBN 0 335 20070 2 (pb)   0 335 20071 0 (hb)

Library of Congress Cataloging-in-Publication Data
Howarth, David, 1963–
    Discourse/David Howarth.
      p.   cm. — (Concepts in the social sciences)
    Includes bibliographical references and index.
    ISBN 0-335-20071-0 — ISBN 0-335-20070-2 (pbk.)
    1. Discourse analysis. I. Title. II. Series.

P302.H67   2000
401′.41—dc21   00-034658

Typeset by Type Study, Scarborough

Printed and bound in Great Britain by
Marston Book Services Limited, Oxford

For Aletta and James

Contents

Preface and Acknowledgements

Recently there has been widespread deployment of the concept of discourse in the human and social sciences, as a number of scholars have used the concept to define and address problems in their respective domains of research. However, in most cases, especially in the social sciences, the underlying conceptions of discourse they draw upon remain largely implicit and conceptually under-thematized. The focus of this book is thus to introduce, clarify and contextualize some of the ways in which the concept has been used in the social sciences. More specifically, I concentrate on developments within the structuralist, post-structuralist and post-Marxist traditions of inquiry, and I put forward an approach to social and political analysis that builds upon Ernesto Laclau and Chantal Mouffe's theory of discourse. In this respect, I focus most attention on the writings of Ferdinand de Saussure, Claude Lévi-Strauss, Jacques Lacan, Jacques Derrida, Michel Foucault, Antonio Gramsci, Louis Althusser, Michel Pêcheux, Ernesto Laclau and Chantal Mouffe, as well as those who have mounted a variety of challenges to this perspective. I also draw upon thinkers and writers who have used this approach to conduct empirical research. The book thus necessarily excludes a detailed examination of a number of related conceptions of discourse and discourse analysis, although it does consider their criticisms of the approach argued for here. These include the explicitly hermeneutical account of discourse elaborated by Paul Ricoeur, the communicative model of language put forward by Jürgen Habermas, the post-modernist account of discourse developed by Jean-Françoise Lyotard, and Norman Fairclough's critical discourse analysis approach. I hope to examine these writings in more detail at a later point.

The writing of this book has inevitably and happily resulted in a number of debts. Stuart Hall and John Hoffman made valuable comments on my original proposal for the book. I would also like to express my thanks to Alan Cardew, Mark Devenney, Joe Foweraker, Jason Glynos, Alejandro Groppo, David Morrice, Yannis Stavrakakis and Jacob Torfing for their comments and reflections on different parts of the book. I am particularly grateful to Steven Griggs, Ernesto Laclau, Todd Landman, James Tully, and especially Aletta Norval for reading and commenting on the entire manuscript. Not least, I would like to thank Frank Parkin, Justin Vaughan and Maureen Cox for their comments and suggestions, as well as Gaynor Clements and Viv Cracknell at Open University Press for their patience in awaiting final delivery of the manuscript. Finally, I would also like to express my gratitude to those students at Staffordshire University, the ECPR Summer School, and the Ideology and Discourse Analysis programme at the University of Essex who listened to and criticized some of the ideas and arguments presented here. Naturally, I take full responsibility for the limitations of the final arguments put forward in the book.

Introduction: Defining the Concept of Discourse

The concept of discourse plays an increasingly significant role in contemporary social science. Although originating in disciplines such as linguistics and semiotics, discourse analysis has been extended to many branches of the human and social sciences. Its growing prominence is not only evident in the increasing number of studies which use the concepts and methods of discourse analysis, but also visible in the widening scope of its deployment. Scholars in academic disciplines as diverse as anthropology, history and sociology; psychoanalysis and social psychology; cultural, gender and post-colonial studies; political science, public policy analysis, political theory and international relations, not to mention linguistics and literary theory, have used the concept of discourse to define and explain problems in their respective fields of study.[1]

The reasons for this explosion of interest are complex and it is not the aim of this book to explore them in any detail. Nevertheless, attention ought to be focused on a series of connected factors. These include a growing dissatisfaction with mainstream positivist approaches to social science, and the weakening of its hegemony in disciplines such as political science and sociology. It is also a product of the belated impact of the so-called 'linguistic turn' on the social sciences, and the consequent rise of new approaches such as hermeneutics, critical theory and post-structuralism following in its wake (Dallmayr and McCarthy 1977; Rabinow and Sullivan 1979; Rorty 1992a; Finlayson 1999: 47–68). Similarly, the resurgence of Marxist theory in the West, as well as the wider dissemination of psychoanalytic discourse in the social sciences, have also contributed to a greater pluralization of the social sciences. Finally, the emergence of a distinctive field of discourse analysis within the discipline of linguistics during the 1970s, and its subsequent take-up by practitioners in disciplines such as cultural studies and literary theory, have led to a novel conception of discourse and a specific way of conducting discourse analysis (van Dijk 1985, 1997a, 1997b; Fairclough 1989, 1992; Jaworski and Coupland 1999b; Willing 1999).

This book focuses on developments in the social sciences, as there are no general accounts of the way in which the theories and methods of discourse analysis can be applied to this domain of study and research. This is especially pertinent given that there is some scepticism about the precise epistemological status and methodological suitability of discourse theory in the social sciences. It is therefore crucial to show how the concepts and methods of discourse analysis can be 'operationalized' in meaningful ways, that is, it is important for discourse analysts to apply their abstract theories and concepts to empirical research questions so as to produce novel interpretations, and to show the 'added value' of their studies in understanding and explaining the social world.

The concept of discourse

In the social sciences, the proliferating 'discourse about discourse' has resulted in rapid changes to the commonsensical meanings of the word. For some, discourse analysis is a very narrow enterprise that concentrates on a single utterance, or at most a conversation between two people. Others see discourse as synonymous with the entire social system, in which discourses literally constitute the social and political world. For example, Jacques Derrida (1978a: 280) argues that 'when language invaded the universal problematic ... everything became discourse', while Ernesto Laclau and Chantal Mouffe (1987: 84) use the concept of discourse to 'emphasize the fact that every social configuration is *meaningful*', in which case 'the discursive is coterminous with the being of objects'. In short, as the concept of discourse has been employed in the social sciences, it has acquired greater technical and theoretical sophistication, while accruing additional meanings and connotations.

As with other complex and contested concepts in the social sciences, the meaning, scope and application of discourse is relative to the different theoretical systems in which it is embedded (Connolly 1993: 10–44). These theoretical systems are laden with particular assumptions about the nature of the social world and the way that we attain knowledge of it. This means that if one is to provide a proper 'grammar' of the use of the concept, one needs to be sensitive to the various theoretical contexts in which it functions. Generally speaking, positivists and empiricists argue that discourses are best viewed as 'frames' or 'cognitive schemata', by which they mean 'the conscious strategic efforts by groups of people to fashion shared understandings of the world and of themselves that legitimate and motivate collective action' (McAdam *et al.* 1996: 6). Viewed as frames, discourses are primarily instrumental devices that can foster common perceptions and understandings for specific purposes, and the task of discourse analysis is to measure how effective they are in bringing about certain ends (Snow and Benford 1988).

By contrast, realist accounts of discourse place much greater emphasis on what they call the ontological dimensions of discourse theory and analysis. Crucial to this ontology is the idea that the social world consists of an independently existing set of objects with inherent properties and intrinsic causal powers. The contingent interaction of these objects with their 'generative mechanisms' causes events and processes in the real world (Harré and Madden 1975; Bhaskar 1978, 1979; Harré 1979; Stones 1996: 26–39). Thus, in this conception, discourses are regarded as particular objects with their own properties and powers, in which case it is necessary for realists 'to focus on language as a structured system in its own right', and the task of discourse analysis is to unravel 'the conceptual elisions and confusions by which language enjoys its power' (Parker 1992: 28). Moreover, in order to account for the specific causal impact of these objects they need to be placed in relation to other social objects, such as the state, economic processes, and so on. In short, this approach stresses the underlying 'material resources which make discourses possible', arguing that the 'study of the dynamics which structure texts has to be located in an account of the ways discourses reproduce and transform the material world' (Parker 1992: 1).

While sharing the underlying assumptions of realism, Marxists stress the way in which discourses have to be explained by reference to the contradictory processes of economic production and reproduction. In this perspective, discourses are normally viewed as ideological systems of meaning that obfuscate and naturalize uneven distributions of power and resources. This means that discourse analysis has the critical task of exposing the mechanisms by which this deception operates and of proposing emancipatory alternatives (Althusser 1969, 1971; Pêcheux 1982; Žižek 1994).

Norman Fairclough and his school integrate a wide range of sociological and philosophical currents of thought, including the work of Antonio Gramsci, Mikhail Bakhtin, Louis Althusser, Michel Foucault, Anthony Giddens and Jürgen Habermas, to develop what they call critical discourse analysis (Fairclough 1989; Wodak 1996; Fairclough and Wodak 1997). For instance, Fairclough and Ruth Wodak (1997: 259–60) use Giddens's theory of structuration to provide an overall sociological framework with which to conduct discourse analysis. Giddens's (1984) theory of society differs from positivist, realist and Marxist accounts in that he stresses the centrality of human meaning and understanding in explaining the social world. His explicitly 'hermeneutically informed social theory' thus places greater emphasis on the actions and reflexivity of human agents in reproducing and changing social relationships. Fairclough takes up this theme of 'the duality of social structure and human agency' by insisting that there is a mutually constituting relationship between discourses and the social systems in which they function. The task of discourse analysis is thus to examine this dialectical relationship and to expose the way in which language and meaning are used by the powerful to deceive and oppress the dominated.

Finally, post-structuralists and post-Marxists such as Jacques Derrida, Michel Foucault, Ernesto Laclau and Chantal Mouffe put forward much more comprehensive concepts of discourse. They go further than the hermeneutical emphasis on social meaning by regarding social structures as inherently ambiguous, incomplete and contingent systems of meaning. For instance, Derrida (1978a, 1982) argues for a conception of discourse as text or writing, in which all human and social experience is structured according to the logic of *différance*; while Foucauldian discourse analysis is intent on showing the connection between 'discursive practices' and wider sets of 'non-discursive' activities and institutions (Foucault 1972,

1981, 1991a). For their part, Laclau and Mouffe (1985, 1987) deconstruct the Marxist theory of ideology and draw upon post-structuralist philosophy to develop a concept of discourse that includes all the practices and meanings shaping a particular community of social actors. In these perspectives, discourses constitute symbolic systems and social orders, and the task of discourse analysis is to examine their historical and political construction and functioning. The approach developed in this book falls squarely into the post-structuralist and post-Marxist traditions of analysis, although I will distinguish and defend it against the other perspectives.

Aims and arguments of this book

This book has five main aims. To begin with, I examine a number of different meanings and uses of the concept of discourse by concentrating on its deployment to ever wider aspects of the social world. I sketch out a movement that begins with a narrow and technical conception of discourse analysis, still evident in mainstream positivist and empiricist research programmes, which is then progressively broadened and deepened by the emergence and extension of structuralist thought. I then examine how the critique of structuralism gives way to post-structuralist and post-Marxist approaches to discourse analysis. For obvious reasons of time and space this genealogy is not exhaustive. Hence it does not include Paul Ricoeur's (1971, 1976) hermeneutic account of discourse, nor does it examine Jürgen Habermas's (1984, 1987a) theory of communicative action, though it does consider the latter's critiques of post-structuralist models and does endeavour to clarify the relationship between post-structuralist and hermeneutical approaches.

Second, I put forward a particular approach to discourse theory and analysis, which brings together three anti-positivistic traditions of intellectual inquiry – post-structuralism, hermeneutics and post-Marxism. More specifically, I articulate aspects of Michel Foucault's approach to discourse analysis, especially his various methodological suggestions and strictures, with the post-Marxist conception of discourse developed by Ernesto Laclau and Chantal Mouffe.

Third, I examine a number of key criticisms levelled against this perspective. These include arguments that discourse theory concentrates simply on linguistic texts and practices; that it divorces ideas from social reality; and that its conception of society gives free rein to the idea that there are no constraints on social and political action to the extent that 'anything goes'. While I show that these criticisms are wide of the mark, I do argue that there are certain aspects of discourse theory which are in need of further refinement and development, and I offer ways of extending the research programme.

Fourth, I consider some of the methodological devices that discourse theorists have developed, and need to develop further, when applying discourse theory to empirical research objects. In particular, I draw upon styles of research gleaned from the writings of Jacques Derrida, Michel Foucault and Ferdinand de Saussure in order to counter the charge that discourse theorists and analysts are no more than methodological anarchists, relativists and 'armchair theorizers'.

Finally, in the course of developing these arguments, I present a series of empirical examples and cases designed to illustrate some of the advantages of employing discourse theory, as well as to indicate areas of possible future research. I also examine some important theoretical questions that can fruitfully be addressed from a discursive approach. These include theorizing the relationship between structure, agency and power; the complexities of political identity and difference; the construction of hegemonic formations; the production of subjectivity and the logic of decision making; and the connection between the role of identities and interests in the social sciences. Let us consider each of these objectives in more depth.

A brief genealogy of discourse

Very schematically, theories of discourse have undergone three significant transformations. Traditionally, discourse analysis is concerned with the investigation of 'language in use' and attention is focused on the analysis of 'talk and text in context' (van Dijk 1997b: 3). In this view, discourse analysis is rather narrowly construed and focuses primarily on the rules governing connected sets of sentences in speech or writing. For example, speech act theory focuses on the fact that by saying something we are also doing something. When someone utters a statement such as 'I promise' or 'I name this ship the *Queen Mary*', and meets their requisite 'felicity conditions' – in other words, they do intend to keep their promises or are authorized to name ships – they are also performing an act. In the language of analytical philosophers such as J. L. Austin (1975) and John Searle (1969), they are performing speech acts. Discourse analysts working in this tradition have elaborated complex typologies of different sorts of speech act and have tried to explain different aspects of communication, such as psychiatric interviews, by trying to identify the intended meanings of a speaker's utterance and the responses of hearers (Labov and Fanshel 1977).

In a related vein, conversation analysts drawing largely on Garfinkel's (1967) sociological method of ethnomethodology, which is the study of the way in which individuals experience their everyday activities, endeavour to deduce from observation what speakers are doing and how they are doing it (Trask 1999: 57). More concretely, discourse analysts such as Schegloff and Sacks (1973) have examined the organization and logic of 'turn-taking' in conversations. For instance, their research shows that a key principle that structures conversations is the avoidance of 'holes' and 'intersections' between speakers. A further aspect of this research has concentrated on the accepted principles that usually govern the logic of 'turn-taking' in conversations, in which speakers adopt certain 'speaker roles' and are encouraged to speak by conventional markers such as body language, gaze, tone and certain ritualized words. According to this particular form of discourse analysis, these insights enable us to understand 'patterns of individual relations between interactants, individuals' positions within larger institutional structures, and overall societal organisation' (Jaworski and Coupland 1999a: 21).

However, in the wake of the growing centrality of structuralism, post-structuralism, hermeneutics and Marxism in the social sciences during the 1960s and 1970s, the concept of discourse has been extended to a wider set of social practices and phenomena. In this regard, the work of Michel Foucault is particularly pertinent. In his earlier 'archaeological' writings, Foucault (1970, 1973) stresses the way discursive practices form the objects and subjects of *discursive formations*. Discourses are thus 'practices that systematically form the objects of which we speak' (Foucault 1972: 49), and they consist of historically specific 'rules of formation' that determine the difference between grammatically well-formed statements and 'what is actually said' at particular times and places (Foucault 1991a: 63). As against empiricist, realist and Marxist conceptions, in which the nature of the objective world determines the character and veracity of discourses, Foucault argues that

certain discursive rules enable subjects to produce objects, statements, concepts and strategies, which together constitute discourses. In his later 'genealogical' writings, Foucault (1987)
modifies his quasi-structuralist conception of discourse. Rather
than describing the historical rules that make possible sets of statements, Foucault is now concerned with the way in which discourses
are shaped by social practices and the way they in turn shape social
relationships and institutions. Throughout, Foucault's approach to
discourse analysis emphasizes the methodological requirements of
such an enterprise, and he is at pains to think critically about the
different strategies and techniques of conducting research.

The third phase of discourse analysis, which develops partly out
of Foucault's various contributions, and partly from Derridean,
Marxist and post-Marxist insights, considerably expands the scope
of discourse analysis, so as to include non-discursive practices and
elements. Fairclough's (1989: 25, 2000) critical discourse analysis
widens the focus of discourse theory to include the analysis of political texts and speeches, as well as the contexts in which they are produced. However, discourses are still understood as the semiotic
dimension of social practice, and thus remain a distinct level of the
overall social system. By contrast, Laclau and Mouffe's approach,
which I shall simply call *discourse theory*, enlarges the scope of discourse analysis to include all social practices, such that discourses
and discursive practices are synonymous with systems of social
relations. In this book I argue for the latter perspective, and it is to
its basic contours that I shall now turn.

Discourse theory

Discourse theory begins with the assumption that all objects and
actions are meaningful, and that their meaning is a product of historically specific systems of rules. It thus inquires into the way in
which social practices construct and contest the discourses that
constitute social reality. These practices are possible because systems of meaning are contingent and can never completely exhaust
a social field of meaning. Three basic categories are needed to
unpack and elaborate upon this complex set of statements. These
are the categories of the discursive, discourse and discourse analysis. By the *discursive* I mean that all objects are objects of discourse, in that a condition of their meaning depends upon a
socially constructed system of rules and significant differences

(Laclau and Mouffe 1985: 107). A forest might be an object of intrinsic natural beauty, an obstacle to the building of a motorway, or a unique ecosystem, depending on the horizon of classificatory rules and differences that confers meaning to it. This idea of the discursive as a horizon of meaningful practices and significant differences does not reduce everything to language or entail scepticism about the existence of the world. On the contrary, it avoids the charges of scepticism and idealism by arguing that we are always *within* a world of signifying practices and objects, such that its denial is logically impossible (Wittgenstein 1953; Heidegger 1962; Laclau and Mouffe 1985: 108; Barrett 1991: 76–7). In other words, using Heidegger's terminology, human beings are 'thrown into' a world of meaningful discourses and practices, and it is this world that enables them to identify and engage with the objects they encounter (Heidegger 1962: 91–148, 1985: 246).

I will take the category of *discourse* to refer to historically specific systems of meaning which form the identities of subjects and objects (Foucault 1972: 49). At this lower level of abstraction, discourses are concrete systems of social relations and practices that are intrinsically political, as their formation is an act of radical institution which involves the construction of antagonisms and the drawing of political frontiers between 'insiders' and 'outsiders'. The construction of discourses thus involves the exercise of power and a consequent structuring of the relations between different social agents (see Dyrberg 1997). Moreover, discourses are contingent and historical constructions, which are always vulnerable to those political forces excluded in their production, as well as the dislocatory effects of events beyond their control (Laclau 1990: 31–6).

Stuart Hall's discussion of 'Thatcherism' in the UK constitutes a fine example of what I mean by a political discourse (Hall 1983, 1988). Hall demonstrates how the construction of Thatcherite ideology involved the articulation of a number of disparate discursive elements. These included values traditionally associated with the British Conservative Party about law and order, 'Englishness', the family, tradition and patriotism, on the one hand, and classical liberal ideas about the free market and *homo economicus* on the other. Moreover, he shows how these elements were linked together by establishing a clear set of political frontiers between the so-called 'Wets' and 'Drys' within the Conservative Party, as well as between those who supported the crisis-ridden discourse of social democracy and those who wanted its radical restructuring.

Discourse analysis refers to the process of analysing signifying practices as discursive forms. This means that discourse analysts treat a wide range of linguistic and non-linguistic material – speeches, reports, manifestos, historical events, interviews, policies, ideas, even organizations and institutions – as 'texts' or 'writings' that enable subjects to experience the world of objects, words and practices. This allows discourse theorists to draw upon and develop a number of concepts and methods in linguistic and literary theory commensurate with its ontological assumptions. These include Derrida's 'method' of deconstruction, Foucault's archaeological and genealogical approaches to discourse analysis, the theory of rhetoric and tropes, Saussure's linguistic distinctions, Wittgenstein's conception of rule following, and Laclau and Mouffe's logics of equivalence and difference (Howarth 1998: 284–8; Stavrakakis 1999: 57–9, 76–8).

Three traditions

Discourse theory critically engages with the structuralist, hermeneutical and Marxist traditions of thinking. To begin with, the structuralist tradition of thought is the major influence on the development of discourse theory. As developed by thinkers such as Ferdinand de Saussure, Roman Jakobson and Louis Hjelmslev, structuralists focus on the way in which meaning and signification are a product of a system of signs. In opposition to theories of language which assert that words and language refer to a world of objects, structuralists argue that meaning depends on relations between different elements of a system. For instance, to understand the meaning of the word 'mother', one must understand related terms like 'father', 'daughter', 'son' and so on (Laclau 1993: 432). Meaning is thus an effect of the formal differences between terms, and not the result of any correlation between words and things, or an inherent characteristic of texts, objects or practices.

While originators of the structuralist model of language such as Saussure were convinced that it could be extended to all signifying systems and practices, they did not provide the resources to carry out such a project. This precluded the emergence of discourse analysis as the original linguistic model could only be applied to the analysis of signifiers, words, phrases, expressions and sentences. It was thus left to later structuralist theorists such as Claude Lévi-Strauss, Jacques Lacan, Louis Althusser and Roland Barthes to use the structural model of language to elucidate a greater range of social phenomena. These included the explanation of the role of myths in society, the formation of human subjectivity in language, the analysis of different modes of production and social formations, as well as the exploration of various symbolic codes, such as cooking, eating and playing sport, that give meaning to everyday life in society.

Moreover, as the original model was extended to cover a greater range of social phenomena, so other writers began to identify weaknesses in the key assumptions of structuralist thinking. In particular, questions were raised about the historical construction of systems, the fixed relations between elements of systems, and the exclusion of human subjectivity and agency from the social world. In endeavouring to resolve difficulties of this sort, writers such as Jacques Derrida, Michel Foucault and Ernesto Laclau and Chantal Mouffe were to question some of the underlying assumptions of structuralism, thus making possible what have become known as post-structuralist ways of thinking.

In the second place, the discursive approach advocated in this book borrows selectively from the hermeneutical tradition of inquiry. On the one hand, discourse theory stands against those positivist, behaviouralist and structuralist accounts of social life that concentrate simply on observable facts and actions, or which disregard everyday social meanings in favour of unconscious structural laws. Instead, discourse theorists draw upon hermeneutical philosophers such as Martin Heidegger, Ludwig Wittgenstein, Charles Taylor and Peter Winch in order to interpret the meanings and self-understandings of actions, rather than pinpointing their causal mechanisms. This means that one of the major goals of discursive social inquiry is to discover the historically specific rules and conventions that structure the production of meaning in a particular social context.

On the other hand, discourse theorists do not endeavour to uncover the underlying meanings of social practices that are somehow concealed from actors, nor do they simply seek to recover the interpretations actors give to their practices. This suggests that meanings reside in social practices waiting to be retrieved or discovered by the interpreter and that once discerned can be communicated transparently from one subject to the next. By contrast, drawing on post-structuralist theories of language, discourse theorists understand meaning as an effect of 'the play of signifiers', and argue that the very conditions that make possible the transmission of meaning – language as a pre-existing system of differences – also render it problematical. Moreover, rather than locating interpretations at either the surface or depth levels of society, they seek to provide new interpretations of social practices by situating their meanings in broader historical and structural contexts.

Marxism constitutes the third major influence on the emergence and development of discourse theory. The distinctive aspect of the Marxist approach to discourse is the way in which ideas, language and consciousness are regarded as ideological phenomena that have to be explained by reference to underlying economic and political processes. It is also concerned with the role of social agents in criticizing and contesting relations of exploitation and domination. However, the models of ideology in classical Marxism reduced ideologies to more determinate social processes such as economic production and class struggle. It was thus left to later Marxist theoreticians such as Antonio Gramsci, Louis Althusser and Michel Pêcheux to try and develop non-reductionist and anti-essentialist accounts of society and historical change. These writers stress the material and practical characteristics of ideology, rather than its purely mental or (mis)representational qualities. Nevertheless, despite these advances, they remain imprisoned within the overarching assumptions of Marxist theory. By drawing upon structuralist, post-structuralist and hermeneutical traditions of thinking, post-Marxists have begun to elaborate a relational and anti-essentialist approach to the study of discourse by pursuing possibilities foreclosed in the Marxist tradition. It is this synthesis that constitutes the main focus of this book, though it is far from uncontroversial.

Critique and evaluation

The theory of discourse that I have begun to outline is strongly contested and has provoked considerable debate (cf. Geras 1987, 1988, 1990; Dallmayr 1989; Mouzelis 1990; Osborne 1991; Aronowitz 1992; Mouffe 1996; Sim 1998; Wood 1998). Realist, Marxist and positivist critiques concentrate on the alleged idealism and textualism of discourse theory, arguing that it reduces social systems to ideas and language. For them, this has the consequence of neglecting the material conditions, institutions and natural constraints on the production and transformation of social meanings. Critics also allege that discourse theorists fall prey to conceptual and moral relativism which renders them incapable of making claims to truth and validity, and/or of making objective value judgements about the objects they study. Positivists accuse discourse theorists of abandoning the systematic collection of objective facts, and of substituting subjectivist and methodological anarchistic accounts of social phenomena. Similarly, behaviouralists argue that discourse theorists' concern with meanings and language precludes a value-free inquiry into social and political behaviour, and entails an over-exaggeration of ideological and subjective factors.

In evaluating discourse theory, I argue that existing critiques are unsatisfactory because they concentrate their attacks on the ontical rather than ontological levels of analysis. I show that discourse theory does not reduce the social world to language understood narrowly as text or speech. Instead, it makes a useful analogy between linguistic and social systems, thus providing a powerful means to conduct social and political analysis. I also argue that discourse theory's underlying ontological and epistemological assumptions circumvent the charge of relativism which has been brought by a number of commentators. However, I do not present discourse theory as a complete and wholly unproblematic approach to social and political analysis. Although it opens up powerful new ways of interpreting and evaluating empirical evidence, there are some important theoretical and conceptual issues that need further clarification if discourse theory is to make a meaningful contribution to our analysis of the social and political world. Amongst these are a series of methodological queries about the strategies and styles of carrying out discourse analysis.

Applying discourse theory

An important aim of this book concerns the application of discourse theory to specific empirical cases showing how this approach can be used to study different aspects of society and politics. As against charges of 'methodological anarchism' or 'epistemological irrationalism', which have sometimes been levelled at the approach, I put forward styles of research that can 'operationalize' its overarching assumptions about society and politics. I also tackle the question of applying discourse theory to empirical cases without subsuming them under its abstract categories or giving in to naive positivism. Moreover, I argue that within discourse theory there is a set of yard-sticks with which to measure and evaluate the plausibility and ade-quacy of the empirical accounts made in its name. Drawing on the philosophy of Heidegger and Foucault, I argue for a complex theory of truth in which the truth and falsity of cases is relative to a frame-work of meaning (or paradigm) within which problems are identi-fied and analysed. Thus it is the community of scholars that forms the ultimate tribunal of judgement in the social sciences and it is the production of paradigm studies that determines the progressive or degenerate status of the discourse theory research programme.

Plan of the book

The chapters and structure of the book reflect its principal aims and arguments. Chapter 1 examines the structuralist model of language and its implications for developing a discursive approach to social and political analysis. I begin by introducing Saussure's structural-ist theory of language, after which I consider the way in which Lévi-Strauss deploys this model of language to analyse social relations as symbolic systems. Chapter 2 draws upon Derrida's deconstruction of the structural model of language to argue that Saussure and Lévi-Strauss are unable to develop a coherent conception of discourse. Instead, Derrida's deconstructive methodology uncovers possi-bilities that are foreclosed by Saussure and the structuralist tra-dition, thus making possible the development of a post-structuralist theory of discourse understood as writing or text.

Chapters 3 and 4 evaluate Foucault's different accounts of dis-course theory and analysis. I begin by considering Foucault's archaeological account of discourse as elaborated in his earlier writ-ings. I argue that this audacious attempt to develop an autonomous and critical account of discursive practice runs aground because it contradicts Foucault's stated aim of providing a purely historical description of meaningless statements. Chapter 4 shows how Foucault's later approach to the study of discourse, manifest in his methods of genealogy and problematization, provides a much more secure basis for analysing the relationship between discursive and non-discursive practices.

In Chapters 5 and 6, I explore Laclau and Mouffe's post-Marxist theory of discourse. Chapter 5 examines the classical Marxist theory of ideology and politics, and evaluates the degree to which

Western Marxists such as Gramsci, Althusser and Pêcheux were able to transcend the limitations of the Marxist approach. It concludes with a deconstructive account of the Marxist approach to ideology and politics, thus paving the way for a consideration of the post-Marxist alternative. Chapter 6 introduces and evaluates Laclau and Mouffe's post-Marxist theory of discourse, and critically explores the approach to social and political analysis that follows from this conception. It concludes by raising and addressing a series of questions in need of further clarification and investigation.

Chapter 7 concludes the book by discussing the application of discourse theory to actual empirical research. It raises and addresses a number of epistemological and methodological difficulties encountered in conducting discourse-theoretical research. These include questions pertaining to the definition of objects of study, the appropriate methods and styles of discourse analysis, the so-called application problem raised above, and issues surrounding the generation and evaluation of evidence. By drawing on a range of existing discursive studies, I show how these difficulties can be overcome. The chapter concludes with a set of methodological guidelines for applying discourse theory.

Note

1 See, for anthropology, history and sociology (White 1978, 1987; Clifford 1988; Dant 1991; Jenkins 1991; Munslow 1992; Hall 1998); for psychoanalysis and social psychology (Potter and Wetherell 1987; Burman and Parker 1993); for cultural, gender and post-colonial studies (Hall 1997; Williams and Chrisman 1993); for political science, public policy analysis, political theory and international relations (Apter 1987, 1997; Dryzek 1994, 1997; George 1994; Hajer 1995; Milliken 1999; Torfing 1999); and for linguistics and literary theory (Coulthard 1977; Fowler 1981; Jaworski and Coupland 1999b; Williams 1999).

1

Saussure, Structuralism and Symbolic Systems

This chapter examines the structuralist contribution to a theory of discourse. Structuralism was inaugurated by the Swiss linguist, Ferdinand de Saussure, and is a central component of the so-called 'linguistic turn', which played a powerful role in our understanding of philosophy and the social world during the twentieth century. The concern with questions of meaning and signification not only prompted investigation into the nature of language itself, but also resulted in the extension of linguistic models into the social sciences more generally. Structuralists emphasize that all human actions and social institutions are best viewed as symbolic systems of practice, and researchers in the social sciences have deployed the methods and assumptions of structuralism to develop sophisticated conceptions of social formations, and to explain events such as revolutions and the actions of states (see, for example, Poulantzas 1973; Skocpol 1979). In this chapter, however, I concentrate on the way in which structuralist theory provides the conceptual resources for developing a viable conception of discourse, and I isolate the limitations of the original structuralist account of social systems.

Structuralism and discourse

Structuralist theory provides an important starting point for developing a viable concept of discourse in the social sciences by assuming that there is a clear *analogy* between language and social relationships. For instance, Jacques Lacan (1977: 147) claims that the human unconscious is 'structured like a language', and the structural anthropologist Claude Lévi-Strauss (1968, 1977) argues that social relations in 'primitive' societies can be treated *as if* they were linguistic structures. In this conception, both societies and languages are perceived to share similar logical structures and features. This means that phenomena as diverse as social formations, political ideologies, myths, family relationships, texts and wrestling matches can all be understood as systems of related elements (see Barthes 1973). Without entering into a detailed discussion of the different types of structuralism at this stage, this means that the individual elements of a system only have significance when considered in relation to the structure as a whole, and that structures are to be understood as self-contained, self-regulated and self-transforming entities. Hence it is the structure itself that determines the significance, meaning and function of the individual elements of a system (Piaget 1971: 5–16; Hawkes 1977: 17–18).

This means that structuralists do not seek to reduce social phenomena to underlying causes or determinants, nor do they treat social reality as a random agglomeration of atomized events or facts. Instead, they argue that apparently unrelated or inexplicable events or processes can be made intelligible by reference to a formal system of relationships. The process of discovering a system of relationships with which to delimit or individuate an essential set of elements is predicated on a new method of analysis (derived from the study of language and mathematics). In brief, this method consists of defining social phenomena as relations between elements, the construction of a possible set of permutations between them, and an analysis of their actual relationships (Lévi-Strauss 1969: 84). Very simply, if we were to explain the game of chess to a beginner, we would first *identify* the different pieces (king, queen, bishop), then explain their *possible* interactions (moving, capturing, checking), before finally observing their *actual* interactions in a real game between two players.

The emergence of a structuralist conception of society begins with Saussure's theory of language. While he did not develop a distinctive concept of discourse, he stands squarely at the beginning of our inquiry. The reason for this paradox is the enormous methodological and substantive contribution he made to the social sciences, and the way he makes possible a discursive approach to social and political analysis. Along with writers such as Marx, Durkheim and

Freud, Saussure stresses the role of social systems in understanding human societies. This focus contrasts starkly with the centrality ascribed to individuals, events, facts or evolutionary processes in positivist, empiricist and speculative approaches to the social sciences (Culler 1974: xii). Instead, Saussure emphasizes the shared systems of signs which make up our natural languages. Words, symbols and other forms of communication require a shared set of norms and rules that human beings learn and internalize. This is also true, he thought, for other social practices and activities, such as playing games, voting in an election, and engaging in civil disobedience. All these practices acquire their meaning, and are thus made possible, if both participants and observers (such as social scientists) agree or disagree upon a set of institutionalized rules. In short, rather than treating social phenomena as discrete and isolated entities, Saussure stresses the overall social contexts in which actions take place and are rendered intelligible.

Saussure's theory of language

In his *Course in General Linguistics*, Saussure provides a distinctive object of linguistic theory. He begins by distinguishing between synchronic and diachronic linguistics: the former perspective considers language as a system of related terms without reference to time; whereas the latter dimension refers to the evolutionary development of language over time (Saussure 1974: 81). Saussure separates these two aspects and privileges the synchronic dimension. However, this does not mean that Saussure disregards linguistic change, as he argues that it is only because language can be viewed as a complete system 'frozen in time' that linguistic change can be accounted for (Culler 1976: 35–45). Without the synchronic perspective there would be no means for charting deviations from the norm.

Saussure's (1983: 15) second major contribution can be captured in his deceptively simple, though revolutionary, proposition that 'language is a system of signs expressing ideas'. Language as a system of signs, or *langue* as he names it, consists of the necessary set of linguistic rules that speakers of language must adhere to if they are to communicate meaningfully. This 'sum of word-images stored in the minds of all individuals' is rigorously contrasted with 'speech' or *parole*, which refers to individual acts of speaking (Saussure 1974: 13–15). In distinguishing language and speech, Saussure (1974: 13–14) is separating: '(1) what is social from what is individual; and

(2) what is essential from what is accessory and more or less accidental'. In other words, each individual use of language (or 'speech-event') is only possible if speakers and writers share an underlying system of language. Just as anyone who wishes to play chess must learn the rules of chess before being able to play properly, so anyone speaking and writing a language must assimilate the system of linguistic rules that make up the language.

The basic elements of a language for Saussure are signs. Signs unite a sound-image (signifier) and a concept (signified). Thus the sign *cat* consists of a signifier that sounds like /kæt/ (and appears in the written form as 'cat'), and the concept of a 'cat', which the signifier designates. A key principle of Saussure's (1974: 68) theory concerns the 'arbitrary nature of the sign', by which he means that there is no natural relationship between signifier and signified. In other words, there is no necessary reason why the sign *cat* is associated with the concept of a 'cat'; it is simply a function and convention of the language we use.

However, Saussure (1974: 65) does not assert that the function of language is simply to name or denote objects in the world. This nominalist conception of language would assume that language simply consists of words that refer to objects in the world (see Wittgenstein 1972; Harris 1988). Such a view would imply a fixed, though ultimately arbitrary, connection between words as names, the concepts they represent, and the objects they stand for in the world. According to Saussure, however, meaning and signification occur entirely *within* the system of language itself. Even objects do not pre-exist concepts, but depend on language systems for their meaning. As Jonathon Culler (1976: 22) notes, the English word 'cattle' has undergone significant conceptual change, meaning at one point property in general, then being restricted to four-footed property, before finally acquiring the sense of domesticated bovines. Similarly, different languages do not simply denote objects in different, but perfectly translatable terms. For instance, Lévi-Strauss (1972: 17–22) uses the French words *bricoleur* and *bricolage* to account for the way in which myths are constructed. However, as there are no equivalent terms in English, it is difficult to provide a direct translation of them, and they tend to be left in their original French form. In this sense, it can be argued that the words in languages articulate their own sets of concepts and objects, rather than acting as labels for pre-given objects (Holdcroft 1991: 11–12, 48–50).

In its most radical form, therefore, the arbitrary nature of the sign has revolutionary implications. Saussure is not only claiming that it is arbitrary which signifier is connected with which signified, he also argues that there is no really existing property that fixes the signified (Culler 1976: 23). Both are fixed solely by their relationships to other signifiers and signifieds in a particular language. This culminates in a *relational* and *differential* conception of language, rather than a realist or essentialist perspective. Language comprises a system of linguistic and conceptual forms whose identities are not fixed by reference to objects in the world, but by their internal differences (Sturrock 1979: 10). For instance, 'mother' derives its meaning not by virtue of its reference to a type of object, but because it is differentiated from 'father', 'grandmother', 'daughter' and other related terms.

This argument is captured by two further principles of his theory. They are that language is 'form and not substance', and that language consists of 'differences without positive terms' (Saussure 1974: 113). The thesis that language is 'form and not substance' counters the idea that the sign is *just* an arbitrary relationship between signifier and signified. This proposition suggests that signs simply connect signifiers and signifieds, but are still discrete and independent entities. However, this would be to concentrate solely on what Saussure calls *signification*, which captures the way in which signifiers literally signify a particular concept. Such a view disregards the fact that for Saussure (1974: 114) language is also 'a system of interdependent terms in which the value of each term results solely from the simultaneous presence of the others'. To explain the paradox that words stand for an idea, but also have to be related to other words in order to acquire their identity and meaning, Saussure introduces the concept of *linguistic value*. He introduces the concept via a number of analogies. For instance, he compares language to a game of chess arguing that a certain piece, say the knight, has no significance and meaning outside the context of the game; it is only within the game that 'it becomes a real, concrete element . . . endowed with value' (Saussure 1974: 110). Moreover, the particular material characteristics of the piece, whether it be plastic or wooden, or whether it resembles a man on a horse or not, do not matter. Its value and function are simply determined by the rules of chess, and the formal relations it has with the other pieces in the game.

Similarly, linguistic value is doubly determined. On the one hand, a word represents an idea (entities that are dissimilar), just as a piece of stone or paper can be exchanged for a knight in chess. On the other hand, a word must be contrasted to other words that stand in opposition to it (entities that are similar), just as the value and role of the knight in chess is fixed by the rules which govern the operation of the other pieces. In sum, the value of a word is not determined merely by the idea that it represents, but by the contrasts inherent in the system of elements that constitute language (*langue*). Here Saussure (1974: 115) compares words with an example of value drawn from economics by considering the case of a coin such as a pound. The pound signifies the amount of money that can be exchanged for a commodity such as a bus ticket. However, the value of the pound depends on the other denominations of money that make up the monetary system or different systems of currency such as dollars. Thus a pound is worth one-tenth of the value of a ten pound note, and might be equivalent to 1.7 US dollars depending on the exchange rate at a given point in time.

These reflections culminate in Saussure's (1974: 120) final theoretical principle that in language there are only 'differences without positive terms':

> Whether we take the signified or the signifier, language has neither ideas nor sounds that existed before the linguistic system, but only conceptual and phonic differences that have issued from the system. The idea or phonic substance that a sign contains is of less importance than the other signs that surround it.

However, this stress on language as a pure system of differences is immediately qualified, as Saussure argues that it holds only if the signifier and signified are considered separately. When united into the sign it *is* possible to speak of a positive entity functioning within a system of values:

> When we compare signs – positive terms – with each other, we can no longer speak of difference; the expression would not be fitting, for it applies only to the comparing of two sound-images, e.g. *father* and *mother*, or two ideas, e.g. the idea 'father' and the idea 'mother'; two signs, each having a signified and signifier, are not different but only distinct. The entire mechanism of language, with which we shall be concerned later, is based on oppositions of this kind and on the phonic and conceptual differences they imply.

> (Saussure 1974: 121)

Thus in the formal and relational theory of language that Saussure advocates, the *identity* of any element is a product of the *differences* and *oppositions* established by the elements of the linguistic system. Saussure charts this conception at the levels of signification – the relationships between signifiers and signifieds – and with respect to the values of linguistic terms such as words. Spoken signifiers are differentiated at the phonemic level. Thus the phoneme /p/ is defined in opposition to other phonemes, such as /b/ or /l/, in words such as 'pet', 'bet' or 'let'. Apart from the substitution of other phonemes, the phoneme /p/ can form words by being combined with other phonemes to make words such as 'pot', 'pit' and 'pat'. Equally, written signifiers, or *graphemes* as linguists call them, are distinguished by the oppositions they establish with other letters in our writing. As long as we can distinguish between the letter 'd' and other letters, we can read and make sense of writing. Similarly, to understand the meaning of a term such as 'mother' requires us to understand the *system* of family terms – 'father', 'daughter', 'grandmother' and so forth – against which the concept of 'mother' can be distinguished. The same would be true of colour terms, in which the identity of 'pink' is only possible when distinguished from 'red', 'blue', and 'brown' for example (cf. Wittgenstein 1977).

Languages thus comprise differences and relationships. The differences between signifiers and signifieds produce linguistic identities, and the relationships between signs combine to form sequences of words, such as phrases and sentences. In this regard, Saussure (1974: 122–7) introduces a further conceptual division between the *associative* and *syntagmatic* 'orders of values' in language. These two orders capture the way in which words may be combined into linear sequences (phrases and sentences), or the way in which absent words may be substituted for those present in any particular linguistic sequence. For example, in the sentence 'The cat sat on the mat' each of the terms acquires its meaning in relation to what precedes and follows it. This is the syntagmatic ordering of language. However, others can substitute for each of these terms. 'Cat' can be replaced with 'rat', 'bat or 'gnat' and 'mat' can be replaced with 'carpet', 'table' or 'floor'. This is what Saussure calls the associative ordering of language and is derived from the way in which signs are connected with one another in the memory (Harris 1988: 124).

According to Saussure, the principles of associative and syntagmatic ordering are evident at all levels of language. This ranges from the combination and association of different phonemes into words to the ordering of words into sentences and discourse. Thus Saussure is able to analyse relations *within* different levels of language, and he is able to analyse the relations *between* different levels, while still employing the same basic principles he enunciates. This constitutes the structuralist dimension of his theory, and provides one of the key reference points for developing a structuralist methodology in the social and human sciences. It is to this endeavour that we now turn.

Society as a symbolic system

Claude Lévi-Strauss (1968: 33) extends structural linguistics to the social sciences in his attempt to develop a structural analysis of anthropological phenomena. He presents four ways in which structural linguistics can renovate the social sciences. It shifts attention from the study of *conscious* linguistic phenomena to their underlying *unconscious* infrastructure; focuses on the *relations* between terms, rather than treating them as *independent* entities; introduces the concept of a *system* of elements; and aims to discover general laws by either induction or logical deduction. In so doing, Lévi-Strauss (1987: 15) applies Saussure's linguistic model to the study of societies understood as complex symbolic orders: 'any culture may be looked upon as an ensemble of symbolic systems, in the front rank of which are to be found language, marriage laws, economic relations, art, science and religion'. He thus seeks to reveal the underlying structures and relationships of human thought and experience that constitute social reality (Coward and Ellis 1977: 14–15).

Lévi-Strauss's project is premised on two assumptions. The first is that there are in principle 'deep' structures underlying the various practices in any society, which can be pinpointed and studied (Lévi-Strauss 1968: 87). Moreover, even though they lie below surface phenomena, they are manifest in language, myths, systems of classification such as totemism, cooking, dress codes, manners and customs (De George and De George 1972: xxiii). Even more ambitiously, he also assumes that it is possible to discern a common underlying structure of relationships for *all* societies. This is because there exist 'rules of transformation' that enable researchers to find correlations and equivalences amongst seemingly disparate symbolic phenomena, just as it is possible to locate common grammatical structures amongst different languages (Lévi-Strauss 1977: 18–19). In order to evaluate his structuralist approach and to examine the emergence of Lévi-Strauss's particular conception of discourse, let us consider his accounts of totemism and myth respectively.

Totemism and myth

Lévi-Strauss's analyses of phenomena such as totemism and myth are of particular interest, because they enable us to examine two substantive aspects of his structuralist account of society, while also charting the evolution of his distinctive concept of discourse. Generally speaking, totemism refers primarily to a unique relationship between an animal or plant (the totem) and individuals and groups living in a particular society. Totemism also signifies certain prohibitions governing the relationships between human beings and their totems, as well as specific customs and practices organized around totems. In some cases, totemic beliefs suggest that certain totems are the ancestors of specific groups of people (Sperber 1979: 30).

One of Lévi-Strauss's chief aims in his analysis of totemism was to dispel the 'totemic illusion', which he argued formed the conventional wisdom of his time. This approach suggested that totemism was specific to 'primitive peoples' who have no capacity for abstract thought. Thus totemism served purely practical needs, or functioned as a source of religion, and represented no more than a stage of human development on the journey to civilization. Lévi-Strauss (1969: 71) shows this illusion to be an attempt by Western anthropologists to establish a boundary between 'primitive' and 'civilized' societies based on the idea that 'primitive' societies are 'closer to nature' than more advanced Western societies.

Lévi-Strauss's alternative account centres on the universal human propensity to classify and organize the world in a meaningful fashion. He examines the way in which different societies use and arrange totemic phenomena for particular purposes, and seeks to 'decode' their signifying power for people living in these societies, as well as those who are studying them (Poole 1969: 16). In contrast to those searching for an essential definition of totemism or for a discrete phenomenon 'discovered' in nature (essentialism or realism), Lévi-Strauss (1969: 79) asks why and how human beings identify with animals or plants, and why these natural phenomena are used to distinguish different groups *within* society.

He also wishes to ascertain what these constructions tell us about the human mind and experience in general.

These two objectives require him to go below the surface of potentially misleading facts and ideological illusion so as to locate a rational and systematic set of relationships that order phenomena in particular ways. Instead of imposing a false totemic essence on social phenomena, and then seeking to explain them causally, Lévi-Strauss (1969: 84) begins by decomposing totemism into different systems of symbolic relations. He then argues that animals and vegetables are selected and used by primitive peoples not because they resemble human beings in any way, but because they consist of systems of differential units, just as human societies consist of different kinship groups.

Totemic representations are thus the means of linking or correlating these two systems of difference: '*it is not the resemblances but the differences, which resemble each other*'. That is to say, on the one hand, 'there are animals which differ from each other', as they each belong to a distinct species and, on the other hand, 'there are men ... who also differ from each other' in that they occupy different positions within society. Consequently, the 'resemblance presupposed by so-called totemic representations is *between these two systems of differences*' (Lévi-Strauss 1969: 149–50). Moreover, these totemic representations do not *express* or *reflect* pre-existing differences, but serve to *constitute* them. Primitive societies are not trying to establish correlations between groups and animals, but use the differences between animals to distinguish themselves. As Lévi-Strauss (1969: 161–2) suggests, 'natural species are chosen not because they are "good to eat" but because they are "good to think"'.

In this sense, totemic classification provides the means for human groups to distinguish themselves from one another. Rather than a unique characteristic of primitive societies, Lévi-Strauss sees totemic representations as the function of a universal desire to classify and organize the world – to establish differences between and within groups. Just as 'nation-states' adopt particular flags and anthems to differentiate themselves, so primitive peoples choose specific plants and animals to mark them out as unique and singular.

Lévi-Strauss's (1968: 208) structural explanation of myths – fantastic and repeated stories that provide sacred or religious accounts for the origins of the natural, supernatural or cultural world –

explores the basic similarity apparent in the great variety of mythical tales across the world's known societies. He argues that myths
cannot be understood discretely, nor as they are told in the various
societies in which they occur. Instead, just as Saussure posits an
underlying system of *langue* beneath the contingent acts of speaking, Lévi-Strauss argues that myths have to be understood in
relation to the series of differences and oppositions that exist
between their constituent elements.

However, the analogy with Saussure's linguistic theory is not
exact as Lévi-Strauss (1968: 209) introduces a third level of language to account for myths. Whereas *parole* and *langue* correspond
to non-reversible and reversible time respectively, in which speech
is the contingent articulation of words at a given time and language
the ever present system that makes speech possible, myths constitute a more complex level of language that combine the properties
of both *parole* and *langue*. This is because myths are not just told
at particular times and places, but also perform the universal function of speaking to all people in all societies (Lévi-Strauss 1968:
210).

Myths are therefore not to be confused with speech or language,
as they belong to a more complex and higher order, and their basic
elements cannot be phonemes, morphemes, graphemes or
sememes. On the contrary, they have to be located at the 'sentence
level', which Lévi-Strauss (1968: 211) calls 'gross constituent units'
or 'mythemes', and he endeavours to explore the relations between
these elements. In his analysis of particular myths, these units are
obtained by decomposing myths into their shortest possible sentences and identifying common mythemes, which are numbered
accordingly. This will show, as he puts it, that each unit consists of
a relation to other groups of mythemes.

However, so as to distinguish myths more properly from other
aspects of language, and to account for the fact that myths are
both synchronic (timeless) and diachronic (linear) phenomena,
mythemes are not simple relations between elements, but relations between 'bundles' of connected elements. After they have
been differentiated and correlated together, Lévi-Strauss (1968:
211–12) can then analyse myths at the diachronic and synchronic
levels. He can observe and establish equivalent relations that
occur *within* a story at different points in the narrative, while also
being able to characterize the bundles of relations themselves and
the relations *between* them. In this way, he can consider myths

both as surface narratives and as an underlying set of timelessly related elements.

Having clarified these methodological issues, Lévi-Strauss's (1968: 230) overall objective is to explore the function of myths in different societies, and to establish their role in human thought and societies more generally. This means he must examine the different sorts of relationships that exist between groups of connected myths so as to discern the 'rules of transformation' that regulate the relations between them. In other words, he must discover the timeless and universal structures that govern the endless production and modification of myths in different societies and cultures, as they endeavour to make sense of human existence.

Deconstructing structuralism

Structuralism has made an important contribution to our understanding of language and social systems. Saussure's theory of language highlights the decisive role of meaning and signification in structuring human life more generally. More particularly, Lévi-Strauss's extension of Saussure's linguistic model to wider sets of social relationships and practices means that society itself can be understood as a symbolic system. Rather than assuming society to be the outcome of individual interactions, or the teleological development of the human spirit, or a product of the underlying laws of economic production, attention is focused on the changing set of signs and codes that make possible different social practices. In this vein, structural Marxists such as Louis Althusser (1969), Étienne Balibar (1970), Nicos Poulantzas (1973) and Manuel Castells (1977) rethought the classical Marxist model of society, in which the economic base determined the ideological and political superstructure, by developing a conception of society as a related set of elements or instances. These ideas provide powerful conceptual resources for exposing the weaknesses of essentialist, positivist and naturalistic accounts of society, while making possible an innovative method of conducting social and political analysis. They also create the means for developing a distinctive concept and theory of discourse.

Nevertheless, there are a number of problems with the classical structuralist model. By stressing the way social systems determine social meaning, it runs the risk of replacing the humanism of existing approaches with a new form of essentialism based on the primacy of a static and complete structure. This assumption makes it difficult to provide an adequate account of the historicity of social systems, as well as the role of social agents in bringing such change about. To put it in different terms, Saussure and Lévi-Strauss's intended revolutionary ambitions are often blunted by their own arguments and assumptions. However, instead of throwing the baby out with the bathwater, this calls for a *deconstructive* critique of structuralism that draws attention to its weaknesses with a view to exploring possibilities that are closed off by the dominant argumentative logics, which organize the structuralist paradigm (Derrida 1981a: 6–7).

The limits of Saussure

Saussure's linguistic model challenges many of our commonsensical beliefs about language. He subverts our assumption that words simply denote objects in the world, or that they represent or express our 'inner' thoughts, or that there is a fixed connection between the words we use and the ideas they convey. Instead, he argues that the linguistic sign is arbitrary, that language is form and not substance, and that language comprises differences and not positive terms. The *potential* implications of Saussure's programme are a decisive overthrowing of the view that language is a transparent system of signs which we use unproblematically to communicate our ideas, and a startling subversion of our ability to be 'authors' of our own intentions and desires.

However, these potentials are not fully realized. Four major criticisms can be levelled at Saussure's writings. He presents a homologous relationship between the signifier and the signified, which together constitute the sign; he fixes the meaning of signs in a necessary fashion; he retains the notion of an autonomous subject of language; and he is unable to develop a viable conception of discourse. Let us consider these criticisms in more detail.

First, Saussure's (1974: 67) conception of the sign enforces a rigid separation between signifier and signified, and proposes a one-to-one correspondence between these two aspects of the sign. Instead of an intermingling between the 'material' signifier (sound-image) and the 'ideal' signified (concept), something that should follow logically from Saussure's view that language is purely formal and relational, he splits the two aspects into two distinct entities and then recombines them in the sign itself. This separation implies that there can be a signified without a signifier, and vice versa. On the one hand, this opens the way for ideas to be located in the mind and thus to pre-exist language, in which case it is only when ideas have to be expressed or communicated that they will have to be represented in language by signifiers. On the other hand, such a view suggests that signifiers are only 'material' or 'sensible' entities that are entirely devoid of conceptuality or ideality, in which case talk of the 'materiality of the signifier' results in a naive materialism (see Bennington 1993: 26–31).

These paradoxes undermine Saussure's claims that language is form and not substance, and consists of differences without positive terms. To begin with, he splits the signifier and signified on the grounds that one is substantial and the other conceptual, even though it follows from his own theory that if one tries to locate a pure signified one only finds other signifiers. Finding out the meaning of a word in a dictionary, for instance, can only be accomplished by being able both to recognize words ('signifiers') and to understand the meanings ('signifieds') of other words. Similarly, the only way of distinguishing between different signifiers is by recognizing differences that are themselves not material but ideal. The distinction between 'bat' and 'cat' is not just a case of a difference between 'b' and 'c'; it is also determined by what these words mean. In short, the logical conclusion of Saussure's own theoretical system is to blur the very distinction between signifier and signified to the point that there is no strong separation at all.

In addition, Saussure privileges one sort of substance (speech or 'sound') over another (writing or 'image') within the realm of the signifier itself. Thus, not only does he separate signifier and signified, he inadvertently privileges the phonic substance (speech) over the graphic substance (writing). This introduces a further material difference within language and provides Derrida (1976; 1981a) with an important entry-point for his deconstructive reading of Saussure. As Derrida points out, Saussure's privileging of speech over writing is consonant with the priority attributed to the voice and reason (*logos*) within Western metaphysical thought since its inception. Writing is thus presented as secondary to speech, and both elements of the signifier are regarded as inferior to the signified. As I shall argue in the next chapter, Derrida's deconstructive reading reverses these binary oppositions and develops a new conception of writing (*arche-writing*), which does not privilege speech or concepts. In sum, these difficulties point to the ambiguous role of the sign in Saussure's theory, and in Western thinking more generally. The sign is there to represent ideas, which in turn designate objects in the world. That is to say, while one aspect of Saussure's writings challenges the dominant tradition of thinking by emphasizing the fact that language is a self-enclosed system of differences and by attributing equal importance to the signifier and signified, he nevertheless privileges concepts and the human mind.

Second, Saussure fixes the meaning of signs in a necessary fashion by arguing that the identity of the sign is a product of the overall system of linguistic values. In other words, while Saussure stresses that elements in a language are relational and thus dependent on one another for their meaning, he presents the overall linguistic system as closed and complete. This means that the underlying *systematicity* of the linguistic system establishes the meaning of each term in a language (Benveniste 1971: 47–8). This results in a new form of structuralist essentialism, in which the system of differential elements is regarded as a fully constituted object, rather than things, words or individuals. In short, Saussure focuses on language as a *product*, rather than a *process of production*. He does not account for the active construction and historicity of structures, and does not consider the possibility that structures or systems may be ambiguous or contradictory.

Third, Saussure retains the idea of an autonomous subject of language standing outside the linguistic system. His theory revolves around the central role he concedes to language users – human subjects – which pre-exist and are external to the linguistic system and he presents the human speaker as the key agent or mechanism which links the sign to ideas and then finally to 'reality'. His writings are thus replete with references to the 'human mind' and the 'psychological states of speakers'. For instance, in his discussion of the methods of synchronic analysis, he argues that '[s]ynchrony has only one perspective, the speakers', and its whole method consists of gathering evidence from speakers; to know to what extent a thing is a reality, it is necessary and sufficient to determine to what extent it exists in the minds of speakers' (Saussure 1974: 90). In this way, Saussure violates his desire to privilege form over substance, and compromises the sharp boundary he wishes to draw between *langue* and *parole*. According to Saussure, the formal and essential system of language ought to be independent of any contingent speech acts performed by individual language users. This provides him with his distinctive object of linguistic theory. However, the central role attributed to the human mind and language users blurs this fundamental division, and consequently many of the inferences Saussure wishes to draw.

Lastly, Saussure stops short of developing an adequate conception of discourse. While he argues that discourse comprises linguistic sequences greater than a single sentence, he does not provide the tools for its analysis in structural terms. This is because Saussure (1974: 125) classifies sentences and systems of sentences as instances of *parole* and not *langue*, thus restricting his theory to the false opposition between language as a total system of signs and speech as a product of the 'individual freedom' of each language user. This theoretical decision means that the construction of sentences and the relations between sentences are attributed to the spontaneous creativity of individual speakers, thus falling outside the remit of a formal structural approach. Discourse cannot therefore be analysed as a regular system of related and differential units, as Saussure banks upon an all-powerful conception of human subjectivity. Moreover, as discourse theory in the social sciences is primarily concerned with the examination of changing and contested systems of discourse, this makes it difficult to employ Saussure's theory without modifying some of its key assumptions.

The sum total of these conceptual difficulties results in an ambiguous inheritance. Saussure's advances towards a relational and non-essentialist theory of language, which can be analysed independently of individual speech acts, run aground because he assumes that both the sign and the human subject/mind can be viewed as fully constituted entities or objects. This objectivism reinforces the static picture of signification and meaning presaged in Saussure's privileging of the synchronic over the diachronic dimensions of language. Language is thus seen as a total system of differences which, albeit temporarily, is fixed; the idea of language and signification as an endless and indeterminate production of meanings is thus broached, but ultimately foreclosed. As more radical critics such as Derrida argue, this is the product of Saussure's insertion into the tradition of Western metaphysical thinking that privileges the role of human reason and thought over and above the contingencies of language use and location. We must now consider the implications of these aporias for a structural analysis of discourse in the social sciences more generally.

The paradoxes of Lévi-Strauss

Lévi-Strauss's work presents us with further paradoxes, as he imposes rigid structural models on empirical phenomena, which he regards as intrinsically complex and historically contingent. To begin with, he extends the linguistic model to the social sciences by stressing the symbolic character of social interactions and structures. However, he does not reduce social relations to a closed system of language, as he acknowledges their contradictory and historical character (Levi-Strauss 1987: 17–18). Instead, by focusing on the way in which human subjects impose meaningful structures and categories on their world of objects and relations, he provides powerful resources for criticizing naturalistic and positivistic conceptions of society. His fascinating interpretations of totemism and myth thus provide vital insights for our understanding of contemporary constructions of identity and difference, whether of an ethnic, nationalist or gendered form.

On a methodological level, Lévi-Strauss provides a sophisticated set of tools for the analysis of social relations, and reflects critically on the problems arising from the study of social phenomena in these terms. Finally, and crucially for the aims of this book, Lévi-Strauss is harbinger of a distinctive concept of discourse for the human and social sciences. The introduction of *mythemes* as the constituent elements of myths differs from Saussure's distinction between *langue* and *parole*, which is confined to the sub-sentential level. Along with purely formal accounts of language elaborated by writers such as Louis Hjelmslev (1963) and Roman Jakobson (1990), this makes possible a distinctively structuralist analysis of discourse, as Saussure's structuralist theory of language can be extended to the analysis of discourses at the wider symbolic level. This approach is taken further by post-structuralist thinkers such as Derrida and Foucault when developing their deconstructive and archaeological accounts of discourse.

Nevertheless, just as Saussure retreats back into classical concepts and assumptions that undermine his first principles, so Lévi-Strauss exhibits many of the closures of structural analysis. For instance, at one level, his theory of myth stresses the endless and contingent construction of myths in society: 'There is no real end to mythological analysis, no hidden unity to be grasped once the breaking-down process has been completed. Themes can be split up *ad infinitum*' (Lévi-Strauss 1994: 5). This infinite construction of myths is replicated at the level of human *subjects*, for just as myths are not fixed by any complete and underlying system, so subjects cannot be certain of their own identities. Thus they are not unified entities standing outside the ever changing world of mythical discourse, which helps to form them, but are subject to the vicissitudes and changes undergone by myths.

However, at other points in his text, Lévi-Strauss (1994: 10) offers the hope of a total and universal account of myth:

> Throughout, my intention remains unchanged. Starting from ethnographic experience, I have always aimed at drawing up an inventory of mental patterns, to reduce apparently arbitrary data to some kind of order, and to attain a level at which a kind of necessity becomes apparent.

Moreover, he argues that myths are caused 'by the mind that generates them' and 'by an image of the world which is already inherent in the structure of the mind' (Lévi-Strauss 1994: 341). The idea of a human mind that is able to generate and comprehend an endless series of myths has important consequences for his conception of social structure. Instead of changing structures that continuously transform meaning, they are split into two separate levels. On the surface level, Lévi-Strauss (1994: 21) locates the richness and variety of empirical phenomena. Beneath the surface, however, he detects a static and essential structure, which comprises the oppositions and correlations between the basic elements of the system.

Moreover, these elements and subjects are analysed as fully enclosed objects, rather than contradictory processes of construction. This is in line with the formal structuralist method that Lévi-Strauss uses, and his tendency to reduce the truth and falsity of phenomena to questions of method (Derrida 1978a: 284). The method itself is predicated on establishing relationships between pre-existing and fully formed objects. Thus his method consists of three basic operations:

(1) define the phenomena under study as a relation between two or more terms, real or supposed;
(2) construct a table of possible permutations between these terms;
(3) take this table as the general object of analysis which, at this level only, can yield necessary connections, the empirical phenomenon considered at the beginning being only one possible combination among others, the complete system of which must be reconstructed beforehand.

(Lévi-Strauss 1969: 84)

In other words, an essential aspect of the method is to define elements *prior* to their combination in particular empirical instances. This means that while Lévi-Strauss seeks to describe the infinite variation of symbolic phenomena, his critique of total structures does not extend to the ability of human minds (both as producers and researchers) to order the world in a complete and logical fashion. Rather, it is this human capacity that makes it possible to capture the underlying essences or structures of myth. Thus Lévi-Strauss pays the penalty of imposing structures and essences, presumed by his method, on the empirical world of objects he investigates.

Lévi-Strauss thus remains trapped within what Foucault (1970: 318) calls the self-defeating 'empirico-transcendental doublet' of modern thought. This means that he simultaneously attempts to collect the infinite set of facts and experiences about myths, while also seeking to *impose* an abstract set of categories or 'structural schemata', which he likens to grammatical laws, on the empirical world (cf. Leach 1974). The question remains as to whether or not it is possible to articulate a theoretical position and methodology that avoids these unacceptable polarities – empiricism and structuralism – while managing to account for their interrelation. Such a desire informs post-structuralist thinkers examined in later chapters.

One final issue concerns Lévi-Strauss's fledgling conception of discourse. We have noted that he proposes a third level of language beyond Saussure's *langue* and *parole*. This level concerns the relationships between sentences, and is thus appropriate to the discursive realm (Frank 1989, 1992: 102–4). However, even though Lévi-Strauss extends Saussure's structural analysis of language to include sentences and the relations between sentences, this movement is not accounted for in theoretical terms. It is not clear, therefore, whether he can overcome the impediments to this development in Saussure's structural linguistics, as he does not provide the conceptual resources for its theorization. More problematically, this nascent conception of discourse is restricted to a too narrow definition of language, as that which is merely spoken, written or narrated, which means that the practical and contextual dimensions of discourse analysis are not explored fully. It is necessary, therefore, to consider approaches that have endeavoured to go beyond the structuralist problematic.

2

Post-structuralism, Deconstruction and Textuality

By examining the writings of Saussure and Lévi-Strauss, the previous chapter evaluated the main characteristics of the structuralist model of language and society. Although it was clear that structuralism provided a vital set of concepts and logics with which to analyse language and society, it was unable to develop an analytically feasible conception of discourse while remaining within its initial assumptions. Saussure's approach is limited to the analysis of language as a closed system of signs, even though he believed his theory of language laid the foundations for the study of signs and communication in society at large. Similarly, while Lévi-Strauss's extension of Saussure's linguistic model to the study of totemism and myth demonstrates the usefulness of structuralist analysis in the social sciences, it also exposes the theoretical and methodological deficiencies of the approach. Lévi-Strauss is not capable of reconciling the sheer historicity and contingency of the phenomena he investigates with the rigid schemas and methods he uses. Moreover, although he introduces the concept of mythemes to mediate between language and speech act, thus facilitating the development of a theory of discourse, this third level of language is not properly elaborated in his writings. It is necessary, therefore, to find a way out of the structuralist cul-de-sac. One avenue is Derrida's post-structuralist conception of discourse.

Post-structuralism

Post-structuralist writers such as Jacques Derrida seek to remedy these deficiencies by deconstructing Saussure's sharp conceptual distinctions between speech and writing, signifiers and signifieds, and by questioning Lévi-Strauss's deployment of structuralism in the social sciences. Let us begin by considering Derrida's attack on Saussure's privileging of speech over writing. Why does he seize upon this seemingly trivial aspect of Saussure's theory? It is because Saussure posits a binary opposition between speech and writing, in which speech is the only true object of linguistic theory and writing is relegated to an essentially inferior and dangerous status. This view is paradoxical because in crucial respects Saussure (1974: 16, 25) equates language with a system of writing, and he also admits that 'the graphic form of words strikes us as being something permanent and stable, better suited than sound to account for the unity of language throughout time'.

Nevertheless, he excludes writing as a legitimate object of linguistic inquiry:

> Language and writing are two distinct systems of signs; the second exists for the sole purpose of representing the first. The linguistic object is not both the written and spoken forms of words; the spoken forms alone constitute the object.
>
> (Saussure 1974: 23–4)

Saussure (1983: 29) also alleges that writing 'usurps', endangers and even 'tyrannises' the privileged position of speech: 'The obvious result of all this is that writing obscures our view of the language. Writing is not a garment, but a disguise.'

The reason why Saussure privileges speech is that sound is perceived to be closer to ideas and thought, whereas writing is at one further remove. It simply represents speech. Even more, speaking always presumes the presence of the speaker and the hearers, whereas writing functions without the presence of a writer or a reader. Thus when Saussure (1974: 112) discusses the relationship between thought and language, he explicitly links thought and sound, even referring at some points in his argument to divisions of 'thought-sound'. However, Saussure presents us with a further ambiguity. On the one hand, writing just represents speech, which in turn represents ideas or thought. Thus writing is merely a transparent medium or expression of ideas, as it is simply the means by which ideas are transmitted in the absence of speakers and listeners.

On the other hand, writing is always able to distort and undermine the transparency of speech and thought because its permanence and materiality, especially its ability to subsist in the absence of speakers and listeners, mean that the 'living presence' of the spoken voice is lost or forgotten. Writing becomes what Rousseau calls a 'dangerous supplement' (see Derrida 1976: 141–64), that is, graphic representations are not just added for our convenience – to represent speaking – but actively corrupt the pure presence they supplement.

In short, Derrida (1976, 1981a) shows convincingly that it is difficult for Saussure to maintain the conceptual oppositions in his theory, as they clash with his overriding intention to develop a purely formal account of language as 'a system of differences without positive terms'. Derrida's critique of 'binary oppositions' in structural linguistics (speech/writing; signifier/signified) is part of his general attack on binary distinctions in Western thinking. He argues that these oppositions consist of a privileged essence (an 'inside') and an excluded or secondary term (an 'outside'), which is merely accidental or contingent. Contrary to the view that the outside simply threatens or undermines the purity of the inside, Derrida argues that if the outside is *required* for the definition of the inside, then it is just as necessary as the inside itself (Derrida 1976: 313–16; see Staten 1984: 16–17). In fact it is partly constitutive of the identity of the dominant term itself. For instance, our ordinary conception of memory depends on the concept of forgetting, as without forgetting there would be no need for memory at all. As Derrida (1981b: 109) puts it, memory without limits would not be memory 'but infinite self-presence'. Forgetting – the outside or secondary term – is thus partly constitutive of remembering.

However, Derrida does not just attack and reverse hierarchical relationships between concepts. He also seeks to construct new conceptual syntheses, which displace the original terms of discussion and incorporate the two elements in a new relationship. So as to avoid repeating the old hierarchies, these new concepts and logics contain a 'play' or 'contingency' in their very constitution and operation. Derrida (1976: 167, 1981a: 90) calls these new concepts and logics 'infrastructures'. Take, for example, the way in which Marxists privilege the role of economic production (the 'base') over political and cultural processes (the 'superstructures'). The deconstructive enterprise would not be content simply to invert the existing hierarchy between 'the base' and 'the superstructures', as this would reproduce the old categories in new forms. Instead, it would seek to deconstruct the privileging of economic processes over all others by showing that this account is based on dogmatic assumptions and essentialist reasoning. It would also seek to articulate a new way of understanding the relationship between base and superstructure – a new infrastructure – that would displace the old conception and make possible a more adequate account of social and political processes. (In some respects, as I shall argue in Chapters 5 and 6, Gramsci's concept of a historical bloc and Laclau and Mouffe's concept of a hegemonic formation move precisely in this direction.)

In this way, Derrida's critique of Saussure's privileging of speech over writing is not purely critical, as he uses Saussure's concepts to develop a new theory of discourse built around the concept of *arche-writing*. In brief, he argues that the inferior characteristics attributed to writing – materiality, absence, repeatability, spacing and so forth – cannot be dismissed because they are of secondary importance. Instead, they are necessary for any language use and highlight aspects obscured by the privileging of speech over writing. He is thus engaging in a transcendental form of argument that seeks to show the conditions that make something possible, that is, he does not reflect on our everyday use of language such as speaking, writing and communicating, but on the underlying presuppositions that enable words to function as language at all. Without these characteristics, no speaking or language would be possible.

Moreover, in keeping with his overall assumptions, Derrida does not just reverse the previous priority accorded to speech, thus leaving the old conceptions of speech and writing intact. Instead, his alternative theory of discourse articulates Saussure's principles of language with other philosophical traditions of language, such as those put forward in the phenomenological and hermeneutical approaches. In so doing, he articulates a new system of concepts such as the *instituted trace* or *trace structure*, *différance* and *iterability*, which form the basis of his new conception of discourse. Let us consider this quintessential deconstructive strategy in more detail.

Derrida begins by showing that all the characteristics of our commonsensical conception of writing are necessary for language and not just secondary to speech and representation more generally. The capacity of writing to function in the absence of producer and receiver, its repeatability and material permanence, and its need to be inscribed and 'spaced' in order to be intelligible are intrinsic features of all language. This means that the sign in general consists of a mark that subsists independently of the subject who speaks or writes it, as well as the subject who hears or reads it. Moreover, it is not exhausted in the moment of its being written or spoken. As Derrida (1982: 315) argues,

> there is no code . . . that is structurally secret. The possibility of repeating, and therefore of identifying, marks is implied in every code, making of it a communicable, transmittable, decipherable grid that is iterable for a third party, and thus for any user in general.

Without these characteristics, argues Derrida, there would be no possibility of communication and no language.

The thought here is that any language is in principle a public institution and resource, which is available for use by a community of speakers and writers. In Wittgenstein's (1953) terms, this means there is no such thing as a 'private language', which can be created and used by a single language user and is thus not in principle repeatable and publicly available. This implies that while a sign gets its meaning from its relationships with other signs in a particular context, every sign can break with that context and function differently in new situations. If I shout out the word 'Fire!', it has different meanings relative to the context in which it is uttered. This arises from the Saussurean principle that signs are relational and formal elements whose significance depends on their difference from other signs. However, this ability to function in different contexts does not mean that all meaning is *determined* or *fixed* by context, as this would simply replicate structuralist thinking. Instead, signs can always be grafted on to a new chain of signifiers or inserted into a new context. This is because signs contain what Derrida calls a 'minimal remainder' of meaning, which enables them to be recognized as the 'same' signs in different contexts.

In developing this theory of discourse as writing, Derrida introduces a new set of concepts that radicalize the structuralist and phenomenological traditions of thinking. To begin with, Derrida introduces the concept of the *instituted trace* as the constituent unit of language. This concept harnesses the phenomenological concern with our *experience* of meaningful objects alongside Saussure's claim that language is a system of differences. Derrida (1973, 1978b) employs the phenomenological method of bracketing the world of material objects so as to focus on their meanings or essences for human consciousness, but he criticizes the phenomenological search for the essential meanings of phenomena and is

sceptical of its strong conception of human subjectivity in constituting meanings. He also queries the way phenomenologists such
as Husserl are suspicious of the role of language (especially writing)
in representing and transmitting meaning.

In order to avoid the difficulties of the phenomenological conception of language, Derrida draws upon Saussure's theory of the
sign, noting how meaning and signification presuppose the existence of language as a system of differences. However, he questions
Saussure's tendency to split the sign into material and ideal forms
– the signifier (sound-image) and signified (concept), respectively.
For him, the instituted trace includes *both* the materiality of the signifier *and* the ideality of the signified. Moreover, traces are not 'sub-
stances', which are present in themselves, as their signification
depends on the effects of other traces. This 'play of differences', as
Derrida calls it (1981a: 26), actively constitutes their identities.
They thus precede the appearance of signs, and function to make
language possible.

If traces become the new components of Derrida's theory of discourse, the concept of *différance* accounts for the active production
of language and discourse. As Derrida (1976: 62) puts it tersely and
enigmatically: '*The (pure) trace is différance.*' What is meant by this
concept of *différance*? In the first instance, it represents a complex
Derridean pun, an example of his word play. In French, the verb
différer captures at least two meanings, namely, 'to differ' and 'to
defer'. Moreover, *différance* is pronounced the same as *différence*,
although in its written form the *ance* enables the verbal noun to
take on a new significance, meaning roughly in English 'difference–differing–deferring' (see Culler 1983: 97). Apart from providing a practical demonstration of the importance of writing
vis-à-vis speech, Derrida is seeking to encapsulate the idea of an
already existing set of differences, and their active production
through the act of differing. This act of differing is also a deferring
of possibilities not actualized in a system of difference. In short,
'*différance* is the name we might give to the "active", moving
discord of different forces, and of differences of forces' (Derrida
1982: 18). Thus *différance* captures the way in which meaning is produced both by the interplay of different traces and by the necessary
deferment of some possibilities not actualized or signified by the
play of traces.

Consider, for instance, the articulation of an oppositional political
identity by a dominated group in a situation of colonial domination.

It is clear that the affirmation of identity x by group y will be differentiated from the colonial power z. This is premised on 'the paradox of identity/difference' in which every identity requires difference and every difference requires identity: 'We are x and not z' (see Connolly 1991: ix). This is quite consonant with Saussure's argument that all identity is differential and relational. However, while Saussure situates identities within a formal set of differences, he does not take us beyond the identity of the system of differences itself. Working within and against the Saussurean framework, Derrida's concept of *différance* argues for the historicity and contingency of identity formation, as every affirmation of identity is also premised on the active deferring of certain possibilities. Hence, in Derridean terms, the production of identity x entails the deferral of u, v or w, which represent other possible identities not actualized by any particular project or discursive articulation. Identity x not only lacks an essence, as it is 'incomplete' and could be different, but its meaning depends on the complex 'play of differences' between itself and those identities from which it is actively differentiated (cf. Howarth 1997; Harvey and Halverson 2000).

Lastly, Derrida (1982: 307–30) introduces the concept of *iterability* to conceptualize the way in which signs and language work. This concept captures the idea that language both presupposes the repeatability and alterability of signs – their iterability – and shows that there can never be fully formed contexts (or structures) arresting the production of meaning. It builds upon Derrida's argument that traces are infinitely repeatable and alterable in different contexts, and that meaning is a product of *différance*. In other words, traces exhibit a minimal sameness in the different contexts in which they appear, yet are still modified in the new contexts in which they appear. This iterability of the sign results in a mutual contamination of identity and difference, in which neither term can be privileged. Derrida's logic of iterability thus implies neither the pure repetition of meaning, which would render us insensitive to the differences of particular contexts, nor pure alteration, which would undermine the recognition of the sign in the different situations in which it was articulated.

Derrida's concept of iterability has a number of significant consequences. It questions a conception of meaning that has recourse to 'pure origins', whether located in the minds of human beings or in universal and unchanging concepts. His idea of 'arche-writing' suggests that subjective speech acts always presuppose a system of language, which continue to have effects on the original producers of meaning after the moment of inscription (Derrida 1976: 60–5). Derrida also questions any simple separation of continuity and discontinuity, as well as the reduction of one to the other. Instead of presence or absence, Derrida emphasizes the mutual imbrication of presence and absence. Finally, his conception of iterability suggests that an investigation of the production of meaning must include the way in which specific contexts transform and change the meanings that are enunciated. In other words, each repetition or moment of inscription is necessarily subject to the distorting effects of context, and thus there is no fully closed system of language.

Derrida's conception of discourse

What are the broader implications of Derrida's work for a theory of discourse? In order to address this question, we need to recall the series of problems identified in the structuralist model, and assess to what extent Derrida successfully overcomes them. Derrida's contribution can be summarized in a series of connected theses. At the outset, Derrida displaces a concern with language narrowly understood as a system of signs, and focuses on discourse understood as a non-deterministic 'quasi-structure' of *writing* or *text*. He thus side-steps the issue as to whether objects are the ultimate basis of experience and meaning, while also questioning the capacity of language to provide a direct and unmediated access to the world of objects. Instead, discourses are 'incomplete' linguistic systems that are produced by the 'play of differences', and which mediate and organize our experience of the world.

This transcendental operation, which focuses on the conditions that make language and signs possible, differs considerably from the dominant Western approach to language. Instead of presupposing that ideas, words and objects can be perfectly correlated, Derrida emphasizes the failures and limits of discourse in representing the world. As signs or traces have an infinite capacity to be repeated in new contexts, each novel context results in the articulation of different meanings. In this sense, signs are contextual and historical entities. Moreover, as linguistic systems cannot fix the identity of signs, and consequently the relationship between ideas, words and objects, Derrida refers to the 'play of signifiers' as the ultimate determinants of meaning.

In this way, the inability to fix meaning in any final way, and the impossibility of completely closed systems of discourse, sets Derrida against classical structuralism. According to his alternative conception, any *structure* or *essence* requires an externality (or 'constitutive outside') to form it. This renders any system or structure vulnerable to the effects of the outside. For instance, as speech requires writing for its own possibility, it is also subject to those contaminating properties of writing – repeatability, spacing, absence, 'materiality' – that are deemed to threaten its purity and presence. This means that it is impossible for Saussure to draw an absolutely clear-cut opposition between speech and writing, and to privilege the former over the latter.

The inability to locate and maintain something that is 'originary', as against what is simply 'supplementary', holds for all attempts to find 'essences' or 'complete structures'. Derrida thus proposes new conceptual articulations or 'infrastructures', which combine the inside and outside in new syntheses. The relationship between origin ('essence', 'inside') and supplement ('accident', 'outside') in these new syntheses is *undecidable*. For instance, the 'logic of supplement' captures the continuous play between 'origin' (thought) and 'supplement' (language), in which it is impossible to prioritize either one of the two terms. More generally, all of Derrida's (1981a: 42–3) new concepts – arche-writing, iterability, *différance* and trace – can be understood as 'infrastructures' in that they embody undecidability in their very constitution.

However, it is important to note that they do not transcend or overcome conceptual oppositions, as dialectical thinking (*à la* Hegel) attempts to do. Dialectical thinking is predicated on the self-movement of 'the Idea' – the development of 'freedom' for instance – and reconciliation simultaneously contains and overcomes the tension between oppositions by raising both to a higher synthesis. Instead, Derrida's conception of 'undecidability' arises from the syntactical arrangement of traces and signs, and no overcoming of differences and binary oppositions is possible. To put it another way, it is not because concepts have multiple and contradictory meanings that they are undecidable; rather, it is the way these words are arranged structurally that makes their meaning ambiguous. Generalizing from this argument, Derrida argues that all structures or texts are in principle intrinsically plural and undecidable.

In addition, Derrida (1988a) seeks to 'fulfil' the structuralist aim of 'decentring' the human subject or agent. Although classical structuralists such as Saussure and Lévi-Strauss seek to break with

theoretical humanism – the view that an autonomous and transcendental human agent is the ultimate determinant of knowledge,
meaning and truth – they nonetheless 'recentre' the human subject
when elaborating their theories and accounts of social life. For
Saussure, language users intend and mean what they say, while for
Lévi-Strauss the human mind generates and comprehends different
symbolic systems, such as myths and totemic representations. By
contrast, Derrida shows that human subjects, whether understood
as speakers, writers or actors in social life, are an *effect* of structures
that pre-exist and shape them. His theory of discourse

> confirms that the subject, and first of all the conscious and speaking
> subject, depends upon the system of differences and the movement of
> *différance*, that the subject is constituted only in being divided from
> itself, in becoming space, in temporizing, in deferral; and it confirms
> that, as Saussure said, 'language [which consists only in differences] is
> not a function of the speaking subject'.
>
> (Derrida 1981a: 28–9)

Finally, deconstruction is not a method in the strict sense of the
term. Derrida (1981a: 82) is at pains to emphasize the singularity of
each of his deconstructive readings, and to resist their reduction to
a formal and general method:

> The incision of deconstruction, which is not a voluntary decision or an
> absolute beginning, does not take place just anywhere, or in an absol-
> ute elsewhere. An incision . . . can be made only according to lines of
> forces and forces of rupture that are localizable in the discourse to be
> deconstructed.

In this sense, his writings are anti-theoretical, as he does not seek to
articulate an overarching set of theoretical propositions, which can
be tested or verified (against experience or evidence) by reference
to empirical cases (as many social scientists do). Nevertheless, it is
possible to discern a number of targets, procedures and strategies in
Derrida's deconstructive readings. In sum, while there is 'lack of
method' in deconstruction, 'this does not rule out a certain march-
ing order' (Derrida 1981b: 271; see also Derrida 1988b).

There are several targets that Derrida wishes to deconstruct and
dispel. These include the construction of essentialist logics and
forms of thinking; the search for the subjective or objective 'origins'
of phenomena and concepts; the positing of absolute historical
breaks or 'epistemological ruptures' in traditions of thought, as well
as the opposite tendency to presume historical continuities; and the

assumption that there are 'fully saturated' or total contexts of meaning. Procedurally, Derrida (1981a: 6) adopts what might be deemed a 'double strategy' of reading philosophical texts and discourses. On the one hand, this involves an initial endeavour to reconstruct 'in the most faithful, interior way' a text or discourse, so as to provide the most 'charitable' and plausible interpretation possible. On the other hand, deconstructionists seek to pinpoint 'from a certain exterior' the 'gaps' and 'points of undecidability' in texts, which enable discourses to both cohere and 'organize themselves', but which simultaneously serve to undermine their coherence and unity.

Derrida and the social sciences

Derrida's deconstruction of Saussure's linguistic model represents a quintessential post-structuralist operation. Not only does he point out the contradictions in the structuralist model, but he also shows possibilities in Saussure's texts that are not and cannot be pursued. Derrida then redeploys the original concepts to elaborate a new conception of discourse. Nevertheless, there are question marks about extending his resultant theory of discourse to domains of study other than philosophy or literature (see Anderson 1983; Dews 1987; Callinicos 1989). In short, does his work 'travel well' when applied to the social sciences? For sceptics such as Michel Foucault, Edward Said and Jürgen Habermas, Derrida's theory of discourse is ill suited to the social sciences, and they fasten on to his assertion that there is a clear equivalence between social relations, discourses and texts. Foucault (1979b; cf. Derrida 1997) argues that Derrida reduces 'discursive practices' to 'textual traces' and his deconstructive practice is no more than a 'little pedagogy . . . which teaches the pupil that there is nothing outside the text'. In a similar vein, Said (1978: 701) contrasts Foucault and Derrida, arguing that the latter's method of deconstruction is a 'textualization' of discourse and discursive practices, which is 'unable to get hold of the local material density and power of ideas as historical actuality'. Unlike Foucault,

> Derrida does not seem willing to treat a text as a series of discursive events ruled not by a sovereign author but by a set of constraints on the author by the kind of text he is writing, by historical conditions, and so forth.
>
> (Said 1978: 703)

Finally, Habermas (1987b: 180–1) claims that Derrida reduces social and political questions to the continuous deconstruction of philosophical texts and arguments. At best, Derrida circumvents issues pertaining to institutional practices and logics; at worst, he mystifies them altogether by considering them as little more than abstract and formal textual structures. In so doing, Derrida erases important genre distinctions between literature, philosophy and the social sciences, such that '*all* genre distinctions are submerged in one comprehensive, all-embracing context of texts' (Habermas 1987b: 190).

These criticisms are apparently substantiated when one reads in Derrida's *Of Grammatology* (1976: 49, 50) that '[t]*here is nothing outside the text*', or that '*the thing itself is a sign*' and '*there are nothing but signs*'. They are also seemingly confirmed when Derrida (1978a: 280) argues that 'everything became discourse' after 'language invaded the universal problematic' and the statements acquire greater salience when allied to his unremarkable forays into social and political analysis (see Derrida 1992, 1994). In short, in Derrida's writings it appears that all experience is reduced to the play of signs and language; social structures equated with 'undecidable' texts; power and exclusion conceptualized as the establishment of binary oppositions between concepts; social agents understood as the mere effects of linguistic traces and signs; and normative questions relativized to the logics of philosophical texts. This leads Anne McClintock and Rob Nixon (1986: 140), for instance, to question the strategic and sociological value of Derrida's brief remarks on apartheid in South Africa. McClintock and Nixon (1986: 140) claim that his analysis of the word 'apartheid' is too general and conceptual, and fails 'to point to something *beyond* the text'. He thus fails to locate the term in the wider and 'changing discourses of South African racism', especially the interplay of racial and class differences (McClintock and Nixon 1986: 153–4). In brief, his analysis is thus 'deficient in any sense of how the discourses of South African racism have been at once historically constituted and politically constitutive' (McClintock and Nixon 1986: 140). (Derrida's (1986) robust reply stresses the materiality of his conception of discourse as writing, and emphasizes the particularity of the context within which the original text – a commentary accompanying a peripatetic anti-apartheid art exhibition – was written.)

By contrast, however, social scientists such as Laclau and Mouffe

(1985, see also Laclau 1990), Timothy Mitchell (1991), Anne Marie Smith (1994a, 1994b), Aletta Norval (1996) and David Campbell (1998) argue that deconstruction provides vital insights into the understanding of social and political relationships. They argue that Derrida's conception of discourse is a crucial resource for combating positivist and essentialist approaches to social science, and for rethinking its foundations. For them, as I shall endeavour to show later in the book, Derrida's conceptual infrastructures and logics, when articulated with concepts and logics gleaned from thinkers such as Marx, Heidegger and Foucault, are vitally important for analysing all types of social and political discourses. Moreover, they believe that the various targets and strategies of Derrida's 'deconstructive methodology' are extremely useful for approaching and analysing texts and discourses in the social sciences.

In the following chapters, I will consider these various responses to deconstruction and post-structuralism more generally. In Chapters 3 and 4, I consider the work of Michel Foucault. Although his different conceptions of discourse fall broadly within the post-structuralist camp, he is opposed to Derrida's deconstructive approach and seeks to articulate a distinctive theory and method of discursive practice. In Chapters 5 and 6, I examine the Marxist and post-Marxist conceptions of ideology and discourse, respectively. By focusing on Laclau and Mouffe's post-Marxist discourse theory, I shall show that Derrida's post-structuralist account of discourse, when joined with Gramscian and Althusserian themes, is indeed useful for developing a discursive approach to social and political analysis.

3

Foucault's Archaeology of Discursive Practices

In the previous chapter I pinpointed some of the difficulties in the structuralist models of language and society, and examined the emergence of a post-structuralist theory of discourse. In the next two chapters, I evaluate Michel Foucault's own particular journey from structuralism to post-structuralism. His writings are important not only because he elaborates distinctive conceptions of discourse in the different phases of his writings, but also because he provides a vital connection between discourse analysis and the social sciences. In addition to articulating an important set of methodological guidelines for the conduct of discourse analysis, he puts forward a series of challenging substantive conclusions about the character of power, subjectivity and knowledge in modern societies. This chapter surveys Foucault's different conceptions of discourse, before examining and evaluating his quasi-structuralist archaeological theory of discourse analysis.

Foucault's changing conception of discourse

Foucault's conception of discourse is paradoxical. While it plays a central role in each of the different parts of his work, the concept remains frustratingly unclear. At one extreme, discourses are autonomous systems of rules that constitute objects, concepts, subjects and strategies, thereby governing the production of scientific statements. In this sense, they are 'a violence which we do to things, or . . . a practice which we impose on them' (Foucault 1981: 67). Thus, Foucault (1972: 47–8) substitutes 'for the enigmatic treasure of "things" anterior to discourse, the regular formation of objects that emerge only in discourse'.

At the other extreme, as against this constitutive view of discourse, Foucault (1979a: 101–2) argues that discourses are 'tactical elements or blocks operating in the field of force relations'. From this 'strategical' perspective, discourses are the means for different forces to advance their interests and projects, while also providing points of resistance for counter-strategies to develop. Thus discourses are analytically distinct from practices, institutions and techniques, but both aspects are understood in relation to more important processes, such as the invidious spread of 'bio-power' or 'the will to truth' (Foucault 1977, 1979a). Hence Foucault (1980b: 4; emphasis added) argues that 'the highlighting, the spotlighting of sexuality didn't happen *only* in discourses but in the *reality* of institutions and practices' (see also Veyne 1997: 156).

These ambiguities reflect the different stages of Foucault's writings. The narrower, though more formative, conception of discourse is the centrepiece of his archaeological investigations of madness, the clinic and scientific discourses in post-Renaissance Western thought. Here Foucault (1972: 135) treats discourses as autonomous systems of scientific statements, and develops a sophisticated conceptual machinery to describe their appearance and function. The more restricted conception is deployed in his later genealogical accounts of modern power, the self and the complexes of power/knowledge, in which discourses are related to non-discursive practices and processes, such as economic and political changes.

Much ink has been spilled on classifying Foucault's writings into distinct phases. Suffice it to say that there are significant differences between the quasi-structuralist archaeology of discourse developed by Foucault in the 1960s, and the more Nietzschean-inspired genealogical inquires of the 1970s. Whereas archaeology describes the rules of formation that structure discourses, genealogy examines the historical emergence of discursive formations with a view to exploring possibilities that are excluded by the exercise of power and systems of domination. Nevertheless, there are important continuities of method and substance. Methodologically, Foucault never abandons his archaeological approach to discourse when constructing his later genealogies. In fact, he endeavours to articulate the two methods in a new approach he calls 'problematization' (Foucault 1984b: 388–90, 1985: 11–13).

Moreover, his archaeologies of madness, medicine and the human sciences, as well as his later studies on the power to punish and the formation of sexual subjectivity, exhibit a surprising degree of consistency with respect to the periodization of post-Renaissance history. For instance, in *The Order of Things* Foucault isolates three major *epistemes* that unify the discursive practices of the West, epistemes being 'the *totality* of relations that can be discovered, for a given period ... at the level of discursive regularities' (Foucault 1972: 191; emphasis added). These periods overlap with his accounts of the regulation and control of criminals and the insane in *Discipline and Punish* and *Madness and Civilization*. Thus the division of history into what he calls the Renaissance (1450–1650), classical (1650–1800) and modern (1800–1960) periods remains constant for his different objects of investigation in both the archaeological and genealogical approaches. My focus in this chapter is on his archaeological theory of discourse.

An archaeology of discourse

The Archaeology of Knowledge clarifies and formalizes the results of Foucault's earlier studies. It uses his previous research 'to define a method of analysis purged of all anthropologism' (Foucault 1972: 16), and outlines the philosophical implications of the 'death of man' prefigured in his archaeological descriptions of the human sciences (Foucault 1970). He begins by clearing three obstacles from the path of archaeological analysis. First, Foucault (1972: 138–40) rejects humanistic accounts of discourse, such as Husserl's transcendental phenomenology or traditional histories of ideas, because they posit a founding human subject that serves as the origin of discourse, as well as guaranteeing its continuity and identity (see also Skinner 1969). These anthropological approaches are bolstered by obvious, yet unexplained, notions such as the book, or the author's *oeuvre*, which are themselves connected by equally unexamined concepts, such as the development of an author's work, the influence of one author on another, or notions such as 'tradition' and the 'spirit of the times' (Foucault 1972: 21–4). While these ideas inform the popular imagination, Foucault argues that they are neither self-evident nor unproblematic, and do not provide a coherent means for describing and analysing discourse.

A second target of Foucault's archaeology is the endeavour to locate a 'secret origin' or real cause of discourse. As against the Marxist search for the material determinants of ideology, or the hermeneutical quest to uncover the true meanings of texts, Foucault advances a resolutely anti-reductionist programme in which discourse is a positive and material realm of 'manifest appearances' to be described in its own terms. Hence his approach 'is not to neutralise discourse, to make it the sign of something else', but 'to maintain it in its consistency, to make it emerge in its own complexity' (Foucault 1972: 47). Finally, Foucault opposes those accounts that seek to pinpoint an underlying essence or unity of discursive formations, because they concede an improbable coherence to what Foucault views as no more than dispersed configurations.

As against these approaches, Foucault is concerned to describe systems of heterogeneous statements produced within a historical 'field of discursivity'. These statements are the products of discursive practices that are governed by historically contingent rules of formation, which are not necessarily available to those practitioners enunciating them. As he puts it in his 'Foreword' to *The Order of Things*:

> I should like to know whether the subjects responsible for scientific discourse are not determined in their situation, their perceptive capacity, and their practical possibilities by conditions that dominate and even overwhelm them. In short, I . . . explore scientific discourse not from the point of view of the individuals who are speaking, nor from the point of view of the formal structures of what they are saying, but from the point of view *of the rules that come into play in the very existence of such discourse.*
>
> (Foucault 1970: xiv)

Differentiating his approach from 'traditional linguistic analysis', which investigates the rules according to which particular statements can be made in the present, and similar statements can be made in the future, archaeology aims at the *'pure description of discursive events'* (Foucault 1972: 27). It thus aims to unearth and describe the *rules of formation* that structure the production of discourses. Before assessing the merits of this project, I shall outline the key categories of Foucault's approach.

The basic conceptual machinery

The category of discourse in Foucault's (1978: 18) archaeological writings refers simply to the level of 'things said', or language practised. It is constituted, he argues, 'by the difference between what one could say correctly (under the rules of grammar and logic) and what is actually said', and the 'field of discursivity' is 'the law of this difference' (Foucault 1991a: 63). Discourses, by contrast, are 'made up of a limited number of statements for which a group of conditions of existence can be defined' (Foucault 1972: 117). More prosaically, Foucault (1972: 29–31, 37) is concerned with particular systems of scientific knowledge, such as the disciplines of general grammar, natural history, and the analysis of wealth in the classical period, or the 'sciences' of philology, biology and economics in modernity (Gutting 1989: 232). Understood in this way, discourses consist of four basic elements. These are the *objects* about which statements are made, the *places of speaking* from which statements are enunciated, the *concepts* involved in the formulation of discourse, and the *themes* and *theories* they develop.

Consonant with his anti-essentialism, however, Foucault (1972: 31–7) avoids the temptation of defining and unifying discursive formations around a unique set of objects, styles, concepts or themes. Instead, he treats discursive formations as *'systems of dispersion'* established by discursive practices, and he proposes to describe the systems and their complex interrelationships (Foucault 1972: 37, 1991a: 53–64). In so doing, Foucault (1972: 38) takes the *rules* that govern the production of statements as his primary object of investigation, and examines the way they structure the formation of objects, ways of speaking, concepts and strategies of a discourse. These need to be considered in turn.

Foucault's discussion of the *objects* of discourse is crucial because it dispenses with positivist, realist and objectivist accounts that reduce discourse to a pre-existing reality (see Bhaskar 1978, 1979). By contrast, Foucault (1972: 47–8) seeks to account for the creation of objects within discourse 'by relating them to the body of rules that enable them to form as objects', and which thus constitute 'the conditions of their historical appearance'. This is significant in that he stresses the *constitutive* role of discursive *practices* in forming and determining objects, rather than the converse. More precisely, he distinguishes three types of rules according to which discursive objects are created. These crystallize around 'surfaces of emergence', 'authorities of delimitation', and 'grids of specification'. The first comprise the sets of social relations in which particular practices or symptoms become objects of scientific investigation and concern (Foucault 1972: 41). The second refer to those authorities that are empowered to decide which objects belong to which particular discursive formation. The last concern the way in which objects are constituted by being located on 'grids of specification' that function to classify and relate various sorts of object by virtue of the properties they possess, or the symptoms they exhibit. As with his idea of formation rules more generally, Foucault stresses the complex interplay between these different rules in forming any specific object of discourse, arguing that rules cannot be viewed independently of one another (Gutting 1989: 235).

The second set of formation rules relates to the constitution of *enunciative modalities*. In keeping with his anti-humanist approach, Foucault (1972: 95–6) argues that social subjects do not autonomously produce discourses. Rather, subjects are the function and effect of discourse. Thus Foucault stresses the need to investigate the different ways in which subjects are accorded the right to speak because of their recognized training and specialization (a properly trained and authorized doctor), the 'institutional sites' from which they do speak (the hospital in which a doctor makes a judgement), and the 'subject positions' from which legitimate and binding statements are made (the empty place of 'the doctor', which different individuals can occupy). In short, for each of the elements of the context which make possible the enunciation of statements, Foucault (1972: 50–5) specifies a corresponding set of formation rules.

The third set of rules are those that govern the production of *concepts*. As examples of concepts, he refers to elements such as the noun, predicate, verb, adjective and subject as deployed by modern grammarians. In this regard, Foucault (1972: 56–9) concentrates on rules that establish logical relations between statements, such as rules of inference; rules which define whether or not classes of statements are to be accepted or excluded from a discourse; and rules establishing what he calls 'procedures of intervention', that is, the ways in which certain operations can be applied to statements to produce new statements (techniques of translation, transcription or reinscription). Throughout this analysis of concepts, Foucault is determined to reject the belief that concepts are constituted by a transcendental subjectivity (of a Kantian or Husserlian kind), or the equally problematic view that concepts are the result of a gradual accumulation of empirical knowledge, in which they somehow map on to an external reality.

The final set of rules governing the production of discourse concern the formation of *strategies*. This term refers to particular theories or themes that emerge within discourses, such as the development of the Marxian theory of value within the discourse of modern political economy. As against the idealist view in which theories emanate from contingent historical events (the meeting of Marx and Engels), or the individual genius of 'great men', Foucault locates the emergence and formation of theories in relation to the unconscious rules governing discourse. In so doing, he refers to 'points of diffraction' in a discourse, by which he means the existence of antinomical statements that are both permitted, yet incompatible, within the same discourse. He also writes of 'equivalent' theories in which the rules of a discourse do not favour one over the other, but acceptance of both is contradictory. Lastly, he emphasizes that not all possible theoretical alternatives are available within a discourse. In this respect, Foucault (1972: 68–9) highlights the effects of other discourses in a particular *episteme* in limiting the actualization of certain strategies, and he stresses the presence of 'non-discursive practices', which can at times play a formative role in the structuring of discourses.

One last, but nonetheless central, piece of the conceptual machinery is the statement. Indeed, Foucault (1972: 114) argues that 'the central theme' of his archaeological project is this previously ignored linguistic *function*. The statement is distinguished from the proposition (as understood by modern analytical philosophers), the utterance or sentence (as defined by linguists), and 'speech acts' (as developed by philosophers such as John Austin and John Searle) (see Dreyfus and Rabinow 1982: 45–8). In fact, Foucault (1972: 97) actually dispenses with the view that statements are linguistic units at all, arguing instead that they are relational entities, which 'must be related to a whole adjacent field' of other statements. In short, statements are not propositions because the truth conditions for the same (grammatically well-formed) sentence can be different 'depending on the set of statements within which it appears' (Dreyfus and Rabinow 1982: 45). In other words, as post-analytical philosophers such as Quine (1980) and Hacking (1985) have argued, their truth or falsity is relative to 'conceptual schemes' or 'styles of reasoning'. In this respect, what Foucault terms the enunciative modality of a statement can be seen to precede the logical and grammatical analysis of propositions (Gutting 1989: 239–40). Moreover, statements are not utterances or sentences. This is because the same statement can be uttered repeatedly and in different ways, and is not reducible to the syntactical structures of grammatically well-formed sentences. For instance, a statement to the effect that 'smoking causes cancer' can be repeated in different languages and for different audiences, yet retain the same form and meaning. Finally, and crucially, statements are not speech acts. While they can be understood as linguistic practices performed in specific contexts, Foucault is not interested in the analysis of ordinary speech acts, such as commands and warnings, but *serious* speech acts (Dreyfus and Rabinow 1982: 48). In other words, Foucault (1981: 61–6) examines those linguistic performances in which subjects are empowered to make serious truth claims because of their training, institutional location and mode of discourse. Hence, in Foucauldian terms, assertions about the prospects of global warming become statements when uttered by suitably qualified scientists and climate experts who present plausible theories and evidence to justify their arguments. In sum, Foucault's archaeological project is concerned with sets of statements that are *taken* to be serious claims to truth by particular societies and communities at different points in time and his aim is to describe the appearance, types and relations between statements, as well as their regulated historical transformation.

The consequences

Four major consequences follow from Foucault's archaeology of discourse: he provides an alternative set of guidelines for practising the history of ideas; he accounts for the ways in which discourse is regulated and controlled in any given society; he elaborates a particular conception of science; and he puts forward a means of analysing political discourse. I shall consider each in turn.

Describing discourse

As opposed to the search for the origins of new ideas in the minds of great thinkers, archaeology seeks to describe discursive regularities. Furthermore, rather than assuming the existence of an underlying coherence of discourse against which 'deep' contradictions and inconsistencies can be pinpointed and 'resolved', Foucault proposes simply to describe them. Finally, Foucault opposes a teleological view of the development of ideas, as evident in what is called the Whiggish conception of science (Rorty 1980: 349). Rather than viewing our knowledge of the physical universe continuously progressing towards complete understanding, Foucault envisages a more complex dialectic between continuity and discontinuity by not privileging either pole of the opposition. He does so by stressing the interplay between discursive and non-discursive practices, and by rejecting the search for cultural continuities or possible causal mechanisms between the two orders. Instead, he tries 'to define specific forms of articulation' between different practices (Foucault 1972: 162).

Rarity

Although Foucault notes with concern the proliferation of statements in the modern period, he stresses their essential rarity. This is because they are regulated by a complex system of formation rules:

> In every society the production of discourse is controlled, organised, redistributed, by a certain number of procedures whose role is to ward off its powers and dangers, to gain mastery over its chance events, to evade its materiality.
>
> (Foucault 1981: 52)

Foucault delineates three modes of control. They are, first, social and political forms of exclusion, which Foucault examines in works such as *Madness and Civilization* and *The Birth of the Clinic*. Here certain discourses are actively forbidden or suppressed, others split unevenly into what is deemed 'reasonable' and 'unreasonable', and discourse as a whole is divided into 'true' or 'false' components, the former being privileged over the latter as part of what Foucault calls a systematic 'will to truth' in Western societies.

Alongside these external modes of regulation, Foucault stresses an internal set of constraints. Amongst these procedures of 'rarefaction', as Foucault names them, are the functions of academic disciplines, commentary and the author. As a result of these inner discursive restrictions, only some statements *count* as serious candidates for truth and falsity within an order of discourse,

whereas others are excluded by the operation of formation rules
that govern a discipline:

> Within its own limits, each discipline recognises true and false propo-
> sitions; but it pushes back a whole teratology of knowledge beyond its
> margins . . . [P]erhaps there are no errors in the strict sense, for error
> can only arise and be decided inside a definite practice.
>
> (Foucault 1981: 60)

Taking the example of the nineteenth-century biologist, Gregor
Mendel, Foucault (1981: 60) argues that though we can retrospectively affirm that Mendel 'spoke the truth', he was not ' "within the
true" of the biological discourse of his time', and thus his statements could not even be called true or false, as they were not *candidates* for knowledge at all.

In addition to the discursive 'policing' of the limits of discourse,
Foucault examines the way in which included statements are systematically *reinforced* by discursive mechanisms such as 'commentary' and the 'author-position'. According to Foucault (1981: 57),
there are in societies a limited range of discourses 'which give rise
to a certain number of new speech-acts which take them up, transform them or speak of them', thereby legitimizing and bolstering
their status and claims to knowledge. The paradoxical function of
commentary is thus to repeat tirelessly a number of special texts in
the belief 'that behind them there is a secret or a treasure', so as
both to maintain their identity, while unearthing something new
and valuable in each recounting (Foucault 1981: 56; see also
Foucault 1973: xvi). If commentary removes the contingency of discourse in the name of repetition, the 'author-position' also removes
the 'chance-element' of discourse by appealing to a unified individual or subjectivity 'who pronounced or wrote a text' (Foucault
1981: 56). Taking an example from the order of literary discourse,
Foucault (1981: 58) argues that the function of the author has
grown steadily, such that 'those tales, poems, dramas or comedies',
which in the Middle Ages circulated in 'a relative anonymity', are
now identified by those who wrote them. Thus the function of the
author is to

> reveal or at least carry authentification of the hidden meaning that tra-
> verses [literary texts]. He is asked to connect to his lived experiences, to
> the real history, which saw their birth. The author is what gives the dis-
> turbing fiction its unities, its nodes of coherence, its insertion in the real.
>
> (Foucault 1981: 58)

A final set of mechanisms, which are neither external nor internal to discourse, constrain the production of discourse by 'determining the conditions of their application'. In this regard, Foucault (1981: 61–2) focuses on the complex requirements that must be fulfilled by 'speaking subjects' if they are to be taken seriously by communities, groups and 'societies of discourse'. Amongst these different forms of subjection to discourse, Foucault (1981: 62) includes the various 'gestures, behaviour, circumstances, and the whole set of signs which must accompany discourse', as well as the doctrines that are shared by groups of speakers and users of discourse. For instance, in his influential account of science, Thomas Kuhn (1970: 23–34) shows how social factors at work within scientific communities, such as personal authority, professional discipline, comportment and informal socialization, are essential in directing and legitimizing the 'normal' functioning of science. Similarly, all these seemingly unimportant 'background' forces are vital for Foucault in explaining who is respected and approved of within a particular 'discourse community'.

Science

The foregoing conclusions about the study of discourse have consequences for Foucault's account of science. At the outset, he does not equate his archaeology of knowledge with the history and philosophy of science, nor does he reject scientific truth and knowledge *tout court*, as philosophers such as Paul Feyerabend (1975) have sometimes suggested. However, his account does differ from traditional philosophies of science, even those Foucault draws upon, such as Althusser (1969), Bachelard (1984) and Canguilhem (1989), because they remain at the level of what he calls *connaissance* – the statements of a particular science (such as modern physics) – thus privileging the role of human subjectivity and consciousness. By contrast, Foucault (1972: 183) accounts for scientific practice at the level of *savoir*, by which he means analysing the discursive rules that are necessary for the development of theoretical bodies of knowledge (*connaisance*). In short, 'archaeology explores the discursive practice/knowledge (*savoir*/science) axis', that is, 'a domain in which the subject is necessarily situated and dependent, and can never figure as titular (either as transcendental activity, or as empirical consciousness)'.

Given this, Foucault posits a hierarchical system of thresholds through which discourse must pass logically on the path to science (*connaisance*). He distinguishes four such thresholds. These are the levels of positivity, epistemologization, scientificity and formalization, respectively (see Gutting 1989: 249–56). The positive threshold is the lowest and simply denotes the emergence and existence of a rule-governed discourse. The epistemological barrier, by contrast, is crossed when a discourse develops 'epistemic norms' (for coherence and verification), which provide yardsticks of validity and acceptability. Foucault's distinctive archaeological analysis of science is directed at those formations that have managed to pass through the threshold of epistemologization, but not those of scientificity and formalization. Thus, it is not especially concerned with those sciences which have successfully crossed the various thresholds of scientificity he stipulates (modern physics, chemistry and biology), but rather those 'dubious sciences', such as modern psychiatry, medicine, and the human sciences, which fall short of scientificity.

Three important conclusions follow from Foucault's archaeological account of science. First, sciences represent just *one* localized type of formation within a discursive formation. They do not exhaust or 'transcend' other discourses, which may not have crossed the various thresholds Foucault designates. Second, while he rules out phenomenological and reductionist accounts of the emergence of scientific norms because they privilege the role of subjectivity or a purely external causality (economic processes, for example), he does argue that they are to be accounted for at the level of the discursive and non-discursive practices which structure and condition the production of statements. The third conclusion touches on the vexed relationship between science and ideology. Traditionally, sociologists and political scientists take ideologies to be systems of ideas or beliefs which represent the interests of groups in society, or as essentially distorted and false forms of consciousness utterly at odds with scientific knowledge (see McLellan 1995). While Foucault accepts that ideologies represent political interests, he does not argue that they are to be analysed as opposed to, or even apart from, scientific discourses. Ideologies are thus not a threat to science, nor does being expressed in ideological terms for political purposes compromise science, because to do so is to view science and ideology at the inappropriate levels of abstraction. It is to treat them as achieved and functioning systems of ideas, and not as discursive practices rooted in the rules of a discursive formation. Hence, according to Foucault, sciences and ideologies may coexist in the same discursive formation, and sciences themselves may have an ideological expression without necessarily compromising their claims to scientificity. In sum, ideologies are a particular sort of discursive practice, coexisting with other practices in a society.

Political discourse

Finally, while Foucault deals principally with scientific discourse, he does make some tentative remarks about the analysis of political discourse. The aim of his archaeology of 'political knowledge' is 'to show whether the political behaviour of a society, a group, or a class is not shot through with a particular, describable discursive practice' (Foucault 1972: 194). This entails exploring the way in which the objects, enunciative modalities, concepts and strategies of 'political activity' are discursively constructed, and then articulated with specific forms of political 'behaviour, struggles, conflicts, decisions, and tactics'. Taking an example of the development of a 'revolutionary consciousness', Foucault (1972: 195) suggests rather cryptically that his archaeological approach would

> try to explain the formation of a discursive practice and a body of revol-
> utionary knowledge that are expressed in behaviour and strategies,
> which give rise to a theory of society, and which operate the interfer-
> ence and mutual transformation of that behaviour and those strategies.

In subsequent reflections on the relationship between discursive analysis and a 'progressive' political practice, these cursory remarks are developed in a different direction. Foucault's (1991a: 69) aim is now to show how scientific discourses can become subject to political practices. He is also concerned to delineate the kinds of relationships that can be established between science and politics. In so doing, he aims to steer a third way between two opposed positions. These are, on the one hand, the view that science is the foundation of all other discourses and practices (being the source of true knowledge) and, on the other hand, a purely instrumental view in which science is simply the product of certain groups or personages (theoretical humanism), or consists of 'acceptable' and 'unacceptable' elements, as determined from a particular political vantage point (for example, 'bourgeois' or 'socialist' science).

Instead, Foucault is concerned with the way in which political practices modify and transform the rules of formation of scientific discourse. This enables Foucault to describe a series of relation-ships between politics and science without reducing one to the other. Hence he seeks to assign the correct relationship between science and politics, to 'triangulate' the relationships between politics, science and other discourses in a given *episteme*, and to chart the transpositions and interrelations between discourses. The latter investigation might reveal the reasons why, for instance, biological concepts, such as 'organism', 'function' or 'evolution', have been deployed so much in sociological or political discourse. From these observations, Foucault (1991a: 67–70) characterizes a 'progressive politics' as one that seeks to transform the relationships between historically specific practices and their formation rules, rather than searching for 'ideal necessities' or universal human subjectivities, which can then be implemented in society.

Evaluating archaeology

Foucault's archaeology hinges on the way in which formation rules structure the production of discourse. However, while it shares a strong family resemblance with structuralist analysis, he does not wish to account for the underlying logical conditions which make certain statements possible, but rather their *historical conditions of existence*. He is, moreover, content merely to describe statements and their relationships, freely calling his approach a 'happy positivism' (Foucault 1981: 73). Nevertheless, there are other logics and tendencies in the archaeological project that run counter to these intentions, and which ultimately render it implausible. First, the logical and theoretical status of the formation rules are fatally ambiguous, and begin to undermine the stated objectives of the research programme. Second, this ambiguity problematizes the role of truth and meaning in Foucault's approach, as well as the critical function of the archaeologist. Third, the relationship that Foucault posits between the discursive and the non-discursive is unclear and unconvincing. Finally, his forays into questions of politics and ideological analysis are not theoretically justified. I shall tackle each of these problems in turn.

Rules, practices and discursive structures

Despite their centrality, Foucault never provides a consistent and convincing definition of formation rules, and their relationship with other concepts he deploys such as 'system', 'practice', 'law', 'structure' and 'regularity' (Dreyfus and Rabinow 1982: 80). In fact, he tends to use the terms interchangeably, since one of his objectives is to emphasize the immanent relationship between the system of formation rules, the discursive practices they inform and the discursive structures that result. However, this does not avoid the problem about the precise character of the rules themselves. This is especially evident in Chapter 7 of *The Archaeology of Knowledge* in which Foucault (1972: 72–4) attempts to clarify the main categories of his approach. Here he variously understands rules to be either inductively established *descriptions* of the regularities of discursive systems (see also Foucault 1972: 116–17), or *prescriptions* as to what can and cannot be stated in a given discourse, or *causes* of the orders of discourse themselves (see also Foucault 1972: 118, 1998: 309). Foucault thus conflates the idea that rules represent empirical regularities between statements, on the one hand, with prescriptive and causal conceptions of rule-following on the other. Not only does this contravene his archaeological method, which is predicated on a *'pure description of the facts of discourse'*, it hypostatizes rules by making them the underlying cause of practices (Foucault 1998: 306; see also Foucault 1972: 131).

Both hermeneuticists and structuralists resist this conception. For hermeneuticists such as the later Wittgenstein (1953), Peter Winch (1990) and Charles Taylor (1992), the grammar of a language, or the rules of a game, are ultimately determined and sustained by ongoing social practices or customs, and rules represent their explicit codification. Social practices are not caused by rules. Rather, social practices shape the meaning and application of rules by providing intersubjective criteria for identifying and evaluating forms of behaviour. In short, while causes determine the nature of phenomena broaching no exception, rules constitute standards or norms that can always be wrongly applied, contravened or followed differently by social agents (Wittgenstein 1953; Ryan 1970: 138–47; Winch 1990). Rules thus provide agents with reasons and justifications for their actions, while causes operate in an independent and objective fashion. Similarly, although structuralists do not shy away from seeking causal laws of social phenomena such as myths, they are wary of attributing causal powers to the rules or systems of signification they discern. Indeed, structuralists such as Lévi-Strauss and Noam Chomsky claim that rules of myth or grammar

are the products of physical and natural laws, which are instanti-
ated in the brains of all human beings, and do not of their own
accord determine the phenomena they govern or regulate (see
Dreyfus and Rabinow 1982: 82–3; Malcolm 1993: 48–55).

In addition to this confused conception of rules, Foucault makes
stronger claims about the overall character of the regularities
governing the production of discourse. For each period, Foucault
(1972: 191) posits a singular and underlying *episteme* (renamed the
'archive' in *The Archaeology of Knowledge*), which defines 'the
total set of relations that unite . . . discursive practices . . . at the
level of discursive regularities'. Not only does this imply a comprehensive system of formation rules governing each 'order of things',
it problematizes Foucault's intention to account for the essentially
dispersed nature of the elements and statements that make up discursive formations. This makes it difficult for Foucault to justify his
claim to elaborate a superior account of the relationship between
continuity and change or tradition and innovation, as we are confronted with a total system of discourse seemingly invulnerable to
external influence.

Truth, meaning and critique

Foucault (1972; 1973) remains implacably opposed to treating discourses as meaningful objects in need of further interpretation, or
as combinations of essentially meaningless elements that can be
abstracted from the changing practices of discursive production.
Moreover, he is interested not in the actual truthfulness of statements (their 'correspondence to reality'), but in the conditions in
which their truth or falsity can be decided. In short, as against the
search for a logical horizon of intelligibility within which to understand discursive practices, he analyses an anonymous set of formation rules that will facilitate 'the systematic description of a
discourse-object' (Foucault 1972: 140).

This view suffers from an internal and an external difficulty. With
respect to the former, Foucault's suspension of meaning and truth
compromises the very viability of archaeological research, as it
makes it impossible for him to identify and catalogue the statements he wishes to describe. Foucault the archaeologist is thus split.
On the one hand, he must suspend the meaning and truth of discourse by being exterior to its production while, on the other hand,
he is compelled to be internal to the statements and discourses he

studies in order to understand their meaning and thus to get the archaeological project off the ground.

The external difficulty concerns the question of critique. As we have noted, a central target of *The Archaeology of Knowledge* is the privileged role of 'man' in the modern *episteme*. Foucault (1972: 130–1) shows that the existence of formation rules forces us to recognize that we cannot fully account for our own archive. We are, in short, radically 'decentred'. Moreover, he also argues that certain statements are necessarily excluded from an *episteme*, because of a battery of mechanisms that regulate the production of discourse. However, to reach such conclusions in the name of a radical archaeological detachment, which brackets the truth and meaning of statements, is to commit what Habermas (1987b: 276–93) calls a performative self-contradiction. That is to say, Foucault's intimation of a radical critique of existing meanings and truths implies that he cannot merely describe the appearance and grouping of statements, but must set out the criteria to evaluate them (see Visker 1995: 41–6). In sum, Foucault (1972: 111) must either continue to 'ignore' the power of discourse 'to be the place of meaning and truth', and thereby risk incoherence, or make explicit the critical values and intentions that animate the archaeological project (see Foucault 1980a: 64).

Discursive and non-discursive practices

One of the more perplexing issues in Foucault's archaeology concerns the relationship between discourse and its exterior. At the outset, the very distinction between the discursive and the 'extra-' or 'non-discursive' is equivocal. On the one hand, although Foucault aims to describe 'discourse-objects' as autonomous systems of dispersed statements, at times he concedes an ontological primacy to discursive practices. Thus, in *The Archaeology of Knowledge*, after dismissing the 'mistake' of 'interrogating the being of madness itself' and 'its secret content', he concludes that 'mental illness was *constituted by all that was said* in all the statements that named it' (Foucault 1972: 32; emphasis added). Similarly, taking the example of the emergence of clinical medicine, as examined in *The Birth of the Clinic*, Foucault (1972: 53; emphasis added) rejects the view that modern medical practices are the outcome of changes in the techniques, institutions or concepts of medicine, arguing instead that they are a product of the establishment of a relation, *in medical discourse*, between a number of distinct elements, some of which concerned the status of doctors, others the institutional and technical site from which they spoke, others their position as subjects perceiving, observing, describing, teaching, etc.

Moreover, as he continues,

this relation between different elements . . . is *effected* by clinical discourse: it is this, as a practice, that *establishes* between them all a system of relations that is not 'really' given or constituted *a priori*.

(Foucault 1972: 53–4)

(For divergent interpretations of these statements, compare Brown and Cousins 1980; Dreyfus and Rabinow 1982: 65–6; Laclau and Mouffe 1985: 145.)

While this strong conception of discourse verges on 'discursive idealism', other passages suggest that 'non-discursive' practices, such as economic, cultural and political practices, impinge upon and modify the rules of formation (Visker 1993). For example, Foucault (1970: 50) suggests in *The Order of Things* that the change from one *episteme* to another 'probably begins with an erosion from outside, from that space which is, for thought, on the other side, but in which it has never ceased to think from the very beginning'. Moreover, in *The Archaeology of Knowledge* Foucault (1972: 45) explicitly rejects the conflation of discursive relations with what he calls 'primary relations'. These relations exist 'independently of all discourse or all objects of discourse', and 'may be described between institutions, techniques, social forms etc.'. He also distinguishes between discursive relations and 'secondary relations that are formulated in discourse itself', but which refer to 'real dependencies' outside discourse (Foucault 1972: 45).

In short, the problem facing Foucault is how, firstly, to distinguish adequately between the discursive and the non-discursive, and then, secondly, to reconcile the determining character of formation rules internal to discourse, with the existence of causal logics and processes that are external to them. One solution he puts forward centres on the *articulation* of different sorts of relations and practices. He thus distinguishes between 'intra-discursive', 'inter-discursive' and 'extra-discursive' dependencies amongst elements. The first refers to the structured relationships *within* discourses between objects, operations and concepts; the second to the correlations *between* different discourses within a particular *episteme*;

and the last to the connections between discourses and processes that occur *outside* discourse (Foucault 1991a: 58). While this solution does open up the possibility of a theory of articulatory practice, Foucault does not develop these ideas further. As it stands, the idea of a system of dependencies and correlations remains too formal, so that in practice it fails to provide a clear division between the discursive and non-discursive realms. Thus, for example, in his suggestions for an archaeology of political knowledge, it is not clear whether his object of investigation is a body of political knowledge, or actual political practices, or the articulation of these two dimensions (Foucault 1972: 194–5). It is to the difficulties concerning the archaeological analysis of political discourses, and Foucault's reformulation of his overall approach to discourse analysis, that I now turn.

4
Genealogy, Power/Knowledge and Problematization

It is ironic that Foucault (1972: 135) never deployed archaeology's 'bizarre machinery' to conduct new empirical research. No sooner had he set out his 'panopoly of terms' than his work underwent an important change in emphasis. The turn to the Nietzschean-inspired genealogical approach addresses retrospectively some of the difficulties in his earlier writings (Foucault 1980a: 64, 196–7). However, he does not abandon the archaeological perspective. Instead, the constitution of objects of analysis through archaeological 'bracketing' becomes an internal moment of his overall genealogical approach, and the two are later articulated together in what he calls the method of problematization (Foucault 1985: 11–13). Moreover, the concept of discourse is still widely deployed, although discourses are no longer treated as autonomous systems of scientific statements, but the products of power relations and forces that form them. As he puts it, 'it is in discourse that power and knowledge are joined together' (Foucault 1979a: 100).

In this chapter I begin by exploring Foucault's difficulties in deploying his archaeological method to account for political discourses. I do this by examining Edward Said's use of archaeological analysis to account for Orientalist discourse. I then compare and contrast the archaeological and genealogical approaches, and examine the conceptual shift from autonomous discourses to the complexes of 'power/knowledge'. Having drawn out the implications of these developments, I then consider their effects on his changing account of the subject, before concluding with a critical assessment of Foucault's overall theory of discourse.

Between archaeology and genealogy

Foucault's scattered remarks on politics and ideology in *The Archaeology of Knowledge* epitomize the difficulties of the entire approach, and they can be highlighted in Edward Said's use of its concepts and tools in his book *Orientalism*. Here Said treats European representations of other cultures such as the 'Orient' as discourses in the Foucauldian sense of the term – in other words, as systems of discursive practice that literally constitute their objects of knowledge:

> without examining Orientalism as a discourse one cannot possibly understand the enormously systematic way by which European culture was able to manage – and even produce – the Orient politically, sociologically, militarily, ideologically, scientifically, and imaginatively during the post-Enlightenment period.
>
> (Said 1995: 3)

More specifically, Orientalist discourse comprises a set of ideas and values stretching back to classical antiquity, and is evident in accounts and representations of 'the East' by Western travellers, colonial administrators and military leaders. This vast archive of statements strongly limits what can be said, thought and done about 'the Orient'. Not only does Said chart the 'invention' of the Orient by European discursive practices, he also shows how this 'will to knowledge over the Orient' provided the intellectual and cultural means for the appropriation of the Orient by successive waves of European colonization and imperialism (see also Said 1993). Finally, by stressing the close relationship between Orientalist discourse and colonizing practices, which together constitute 'a science of imperialism', he also emphasizes the general complicity of all knowledge and political institutions and practices (Young 1990: 126–7).

Said's deployment of Foucault's conception of discourse highlights a series of contradictions in the archaeological project. One difficulty concerns the ontological status of Orientalist discourse. Does it comprise a system of texts and statements that represent the Orient, or does it perform the more constructive role of actually *bringing into existence* the object it describes? Said's answer is ambivalent. On the one hand, Orientalism 'is a *system of representations* framed by a whole set of forces that brought the Orient into Western learning' (Said 1995: 202–3; emphasis added). Thus

> the phenomenon of Orientalism ... deals principally, not with a correspondence between Orientalism and Orient, but with the *internal consistency of Orientalism and its ideas* about the Orient ... despite or beyond any correspondence, or lack thereof, with a 'real' Orient.
>
> (Said 1995: 5; emphasis added)

On the other hand, however, especially after the failure of Napoleon's occupation of Egypt, 'the very language of Orientialism changed radically ... and became not merely a style of representation but a language, indeed a means of *creation*' (Said 1995: 87). In this conception, Orientalist texts '*create* not only knowledge but also the very reality they appear to describe' (Said 1995: 94).

This ontological ambiguity has consequences for Said's epistemology. If he is to remain faithful to a representational conception of knowledge he must assume, first, that there is something to be represented and, second, that these representations either represent or misrepresent social reality. If, by contrast, Said adopts the constructivist or conventional theory of knowledge, then he need not adhere to these commitments, as Orientalist discourse would produce its own object of analysis with its own criteria of truth and falsity. In the latter case, however, the category of representation itself is jeopardized, as Said (1995: 272; emphasis added) half recognizes when he argues that

> [s]ince Islam *has* been fundamentally misrepresented in the West[,] *the real issue is whether indeed there can be a true representation of anything*, or whether any and all representations, are embedded first in the language and then in the culture, institutions, and political ambience of the representer.

Nevertheless, despite these misgivings, Said never spells out the full implications of this thought, and his reference to the 'misrepresentation' of Islam in the West itself undercuts the very reservations to which he alludes. It has thus been left to writers such as Timothy Mitchell (1991: 32) to argue that the question of representation and misrepresentation is misleading, and that the important consideration is to

> understand how the West had come to live as though the world were divided ... into a realm of representations and a realm of 'the real';

into exhibitions and an external reality; into an order of mere models, descriptions or copies, and an order of the original.

In other words, from this perspective the key issue is to grasp how the division of the social world into 'representations' and 'reality' was an effect of modern Western discursive practices.

Said's difficulties in this regard echo the problems in Foucault's archaeological conception of discourse. The first concerns the relationship between discourses and the realities they claim to represent. Although Foucault is entitled to question realist accounts of science, in which discourses reflect a pre-existing world of objects, he never satisfactorily explains the relationship between discursive objects and the statements made about them, on the one hand, and the real objects they describe on the other. The fatal consequences of this equivocation are evident in Said's vacillations about Orientalist discourse.

The second concerns the thorny relationship between discursive and non-discursive practices. Although Said wishes to show the material and political effects of discursive practices on the construction of the 'Occidental self' and the 'Oriental other', as well as the organic connection between Orientalist discourse and Western power, it is not clear how this articulation is understood. Put bluntly, Said is unable to reconcile the way in which Orientalist discourse is a pure discursive fabrication, utterly divorced from the reality it claims to represent, yet still facilitates the conquest, restructuring and administration of the 'actual' Orient (Young 1990: 129).

Finally, although Said is heavily critical of Orientalism and its consequences for the relationships between 'East' and 'West', he does not provide a plausible justification of such a critique. It rests primarily on the affirmation of universal 'humanistic values', and the defence of 'human experience', which he argues are systematically denied by the functioning of Orientalist discourse (Said 1995: 110, 266). Hence the ethical questions raised by the division of 'human reality' into 'clearly different cultures, histories, traditions, societies, even races' concern the degree to which they can be survived 'humanly', that is, by avoiding their being hardened into 'them' and 'us' categorizations (Said 1995: 45–6). In addition, Said (1995: 326) posits the role of the intellectual as an 'independent critical consciousness' who can draw upon an authentic human experience to oppose the anti-humanist ideology of Orientalism. In so doing, he articulates Foucault's concept of a 'specific', rather than 'universal', intellectual to capture the 'imprint' of each individual's agency in formulating and criticizing Orientalist discourse (Said 1995: 23; see also Said 1975: 279–315).

However, Said's basis of critique is problematical in a number of respects. The very universal values that he invokes are themselves products of the Western discourses he sees as essentially complicit with Orientalism. Moreover, at least part of Said's project is surely to affirm the particularity and heterogeneity of different cultures, and not reduce them to some abstract universality. However, it is not clear how Said can bring about this pluralistic conception of cultures and discourses while still retaining the notion of a universal human experience. Finally, while Said stresses the role of the 'specific intellectual' as a critic of the totalizing system of Orientalist discourse, it is unclear how his conception of the intellectual is not itself universalistic. Said's account seems uncomfortably close to Karl Mannheim's (1936) conception of the universal intellectual who, as a privileged subject of knowledge, is able to criticize ideological systems in a neutral fashion. It is in response to these problems in the archaeological method that Foucault was to develop his genealogical approach.

Archaeology, genealogy and problematization

Foucault's genealogy (1987: 77) continues his assault on 'traditional' history begun in *The Archaeology of Knowledge* by opposing the search for 'ideal significations and indefinite teleologies' in the study of history. Instead of searching for underlying origins and metaphysical essences, he focuses on the 'ignoble beginnings' and the contingent fabrications of historical phenomena. Thus he investigates the unpredictable events that form entities, and stresses the eruption of clashing political forces in key historical conjunctures as the driving element of history. Moreover, while traditional historians adopt a 'suprahistorical' point of view, taking history to be an objective process separate from the historian's gaze, genealogy is committed to a thoroughgoing 'perspectivism' in which events are perceived from the particular point of view of a 'situated' researcher. Foucault's (1987: 87–8) 'effective history' thus entails a radical historicization of discourses, institutions and practices, such that '[n]othing in man – not even his body – is sufficiently stable to serve as the basis for self-recognition or for understanding other men'.

This sets up a series of contrasts between Foucault's archaeological and genealogical methods. First, whereas the archaeologist wears the mask of a spectator who simply describes discourses, the genealogist diagnoses and offers cures for the problems of contemporary societies by examining their historical emergence and formation. Instead of the 'happy positivist' charting the appearance and regularity of statements, Foucault is now an engaged critic of the discourses he explores. Second, while the archaeologist suspends the values of truth, knowledge and meaning, the genealogist recognizes the impossibility of avoiding these questions, even if truth and knowledge cannot be accepted at face value, or deployed unproblematically in the name of freedom and the critique of power. For Foucault (1987: 72) the genealogist, 'truth isn't outside power, or lacking in power', but 'a thing of this world', which must be internally connected with logics of power and domination. Finally, while the archaeologist studies discourses as autonomous rule-governed practices, the genealogist produces 'a form of history which can account for the constitution of knowledges, discourses, domains of objects' that necessarily involves the complex interaction of discursive and non-discursive practices (Foucault 1980a: 117). Genealogy is thus explicitly concerned with the centrality of power and domination in the constitution of discourses, identities and institutions and involves the adoption of a critical ethos toward them (see Owen 1994: 210–13; Tully 1999).

Foucault (1977, 1979a) deploys his genealogical method in a number of important studies to account for the invidious spread of power, regulation and control in modern societies. From these studies, it is possible to formalize the underlying methods and concepts of his genealogical approach. The first step is the diagnosis of the problem that engenders each genealogical reading. For example, at the beginning of *Discipline and Punish*, Foucault (1977: 23) argues that his study is '*a genealogy of the present scientifico-legal complex* from which the power to punish derives its bases, justifications and rules', and he goes on to argue that his concern with punishment and the prison emerges 'not so much from history as from the present'. This does not involve a presentist or teleological conception of history, in which the historian understands the past in terms of the present, or sees in the past the origins of the present. Instead, it begins with the problematization of an issue confronting the historian in society, and then seeks to examine its contingent historical and political emergence. The genealogist thus seeks to uncover the 'lowly origins' and 'play of dominations' that produced the phenomenon, while also showing possibilities excluded by the dominant logics of historical development. In this way, the genealogist discloses new possibilities foreclosed by existing interpretations.

The 'repressive hypothesis'

One such issue is the 'repressive hypothesis', which Foucault (1979a: 15–49) introduces at the start of the first volume of *The History of Sexuality* and then connects to his alternative interpretation of modernity. By introducing the repressive hypothesis, Foucault posits a paradigmatic conception of the relationship between truth, power, sexuality and the body. Historically, he argues, this picture suggests that European history undergoes a movement from a 'lively frankness' about sexuality in the classical period, to a growing repression and silencing of sexual discourse and practices in the modern period, especially during the hegemony of the Victorian bourgeoisie. This period is then 'liberated' by the new discourses and practices associated with the post-modern period of sexual freedom (Foucault 1979a: 3–4).

In place of these discontinuities, Foucault stresses an increasing 'proliferation of discourse' about sex during the eighteenth and nineteenth centuries. He argues (Foucault 1979a: 18) that the supposed Victorian repression of sexuality was only made possible by 'an institutional incitement to speak about it, and to do so more and more; a determination on the part of the agencies of power to hear it spoken about, and to cause *it* to speak through explicit articulation and endlessly accumulated detail'. According to Foucault (1979a: 23), this 'constant optimization' and 'increasing valorization of the discourse on sex' – the 'transformation of sex into discourse' (Foucault 1979a: 36) – had a number of significant aims and effects. In the first place, even if the avowed aim of the Victorians was to regulate sexual practices, the means employed resulted in what Foucault (1979a: 37) calls 'a multiplication of "perversions"', as a variety of 'unnatural' (Foucault 1979a: 39) behaviours and polymorphous pleasures were discursively constructed, that is, 'drawn out, revealed, isolated, intensified, incorporated, by multifarious power devices' (Foucault 1979a: 48). This 'perverse implantation' is part of a general 'medicalization' of sexuality, in which a new set of discursive practices – a *'scienta sexualis'* – emerges around an empirical and 'natural' object of scientific knowledge (McNay 1994: 96). In this way, sexual pleasures and activities become an important means of accessing the truth about the nature and 'essence' of human beings. They become what Foucault (1979a: 69) calls, borrowing from Nietzsche, a central part of the growing 'will to truth' in Western societies.

Foucault gives a number of reasons for the emergence and strength of the repressive hypothesis in modern Western thinking. First, it bolsters an account of history in which the development of capitalist social relations is conceded a primary role, and discourses of sexuality are seen as merely functional to the overarching needs of capitalist production and reproduction. Second, it implies that discourses and practices of sexuality can challenge dominant economic logics and political power in the name of freedom and liberation. Most importantly, however, is the way in which the repressive hypothesis is rooted in what he calls the 'juridico-discursive' conception of power, which is the predominant understanding of power in Western societies. In this legalistic conception, power is seen to constrain freedom by repression and prohibitions, such that the production of truth and knowledge can be seen to challenge power in the name of greater freedom or sexual licence. This model is attractive because it benefits those intellectuals and protesters who speak out against power and domination in the name of a universal truth or reason, and it bolsters the prevailing understandings of power in liberal democratic regimes (Foucault 1979a: 6, 86–8).

However, for Foucault (1979a: 86) this perspective conceals and makes tolerable the more insidious forms of power by which social relations are organized, ordered and regulated. The juridico-discursive model thus fails to examine what he calls the 'normalizing functions' and 'disciplinary technologies' of power, which are directed at the production of 'docile bodies' (Foucault 1977: 138). In other words, it fails to detect the operation of power that organizes, controls and regulates the human body in ways that are suitable for the reproduction of capitalist relations of production in factories and workshops, and for the operation of institutions such as schools, armies, hospitals and prisons (see Mitchell 1991). Foucault (1977: 194) thus proposes a productive conception of power in which power and 'true' discourses about sexuality are not opposed, but interconnected or immanent.

Bio-power

In specifying the repressive hypothesis, Foucault isolates an important paradigm of power, knowledge, sexuality and the body. Moreover, he argues that this apparatus or *dispositif* both structures the
beliefs of those analysing and challenging systems of power in the
name of liberation, and is immanent in the practices governing
modern society. As a genealogist, his task is to expose the deception
of the repressive hypothesis, without relying on a model of false
consciousness, and without reducing this apparatus to an underlying causal logic that determines its character and operation.
Foucault does this by connecting the repressive hypothesis to a
genealogy of the emergence and formation of what he calls 'bio-
power', thus relativizing and revealing its function in relation to it.

Bio-power is defined by Foucault (1979a: 140) as an increasing
'subjugation of bodies and . . . control of populations' for the sake
of generating greater utility, efficiency and productivity. While he
traces the emergence of this new form of power back to the Greek
polis, it is not until the classical period that the new logic begins to
take hold and assume greater centrality (1979a: 140). Foucault concentrates on two dimensions of its operation. These are a general
concern by governors and administrators of states with the human
species as a whole – for instance, the biological risks confronting
the species or the size of populations – and a 'micro-physics' of the
body, in which the aim of power is to train and discipline human
bodies in ways that are conducive to their greater organization and
productivity.

In more political terms, Foucault captures these logics with his
ideas of 'governmentality' and 'pastoral power', respectively. In
opposition to monarchical and contractual conceptions of government, governmentality is not concerned with 'territory but rather a
sort of complex composed of men and things'. Government is thus
concerned with men in their multifarious social and economic
relationships (wealth, resources, means of subsistence, territory);
their cultural and symbolic interactions (customs, habits, ways of
acting); and their relation to 'the accidents and misfortunes of social
existence' (Foucault 1991a: 93). 'Pastoralism', by contrast, is a particular technique of governmentality, and Foucault (1988: 77–8)
examines the development of 'policing' to illustrate his different
perspective on questions of governance. In brief, the object of the
latter is not simply to enforce power and law, but to cultivate

'modesty, charity, loyalty, industriousness, friendly co-operation, honesty' amongst the subjects of a state.

In the modern period, these two dimensions of bio-power are articulated together around sex, which becomes a nodal point for its dissemination. Thus the proliferation of discourses around sexuality, which Foucault locates in the rise of confessional technologies, results in the linking together of concerns with the body and the species. Thus, in contrast to a supposed asceticism accompanying the rise of capitalism, Foucault (1979a: 123) posits 'an intensification of the body, a problematization of health and its operational terms', which became part of an apparatus directed at 'techniques for maximizing life'. In this respect, the 'primary concern was not the repression of the sex of classes to be exploited, but rather the body, vigor, longevity, progeniture, and descent of the classes that "ruled"'. Moreover, by the nineteenth century, this 'deployment of sexuality' had spread throughout society. Hence,

> the nineteenth century witnessed a generalization of the deployment of sexuality, starting from a hegemonic centre. Eventually the entire social body was provided with a 'sexual body', although this was accomplished in different ways and using different tools.
>
> (Foucault 1979a: 127)

In sum, Foucault's questioning of and genealogical accounting for the 'repressive hypothesis' in relation to bio-power suggest that the repressive hypothesis functioned as a mask to conceal the operation of more profound and far-reaching changes to modern Western societies. It thus became the conduit for the effective dissemination of bio-power. From this perspective, the repressive hypothesis and the confessional are not mutually contradictory and exclusionary, but two sides of the same coin. They contribute, rather, to the emergence and functioning of normalizing power, and both are subjected to genealogical critique.

It is necessary to stress three important caveats to the genealogical approach, which Foucault deploys to relativize and criticize the repressive hypothesis. Firstly, it does not give rise to arbitrary constructions that bear no resemblance to history. On the contrary, while motivated by problems diagnosed in our contemporary condition, genealogy seeks to provide a more plausible narrative of historical processes by viewing them from their proper perspective. These vantage-points are shaped by the dominant logics of our present situation. Secondly, Foucault has no recourse to the totalizing or humanistic accounts of history that he criticizes in both the archaeological and genealogical phases of his writings. Lastly, Foucault does not offer purely subjectivistic or nihilistic accounts of the phenomena he investigates, though the interpretations he proffers may be criticized for their historical accuracy and perspicacity. Foucault is not denying historical facts in the name of personal whimsy, but only the importance of interpreting and contextualizing the facts he presents. Thus his accounts are both critical and evaluative of the logics of bio-power and subjectivity that are at the centre of his interpretations. In short, while *Discipline and Punish* provides a critique of the objectification of human beings by 'disciplinary power', *The History of Sexuality* is critical of the way in which modern bio-power induces humans to 'subjectify' themselves by specific confessional technologies and ethical practices of the self (Dreyfus and Rabinow 1982: 126–7).

Discourse, power/knowledge and ideology

From the brief overview of Foucault's problematization of bio-power, it is possible to discern a clear shift in his conceptualization of discourse. Foucault (1977: 27) replaces the view that discourses are autonomous systems of statements structured by historically specific formation rules, with particular systems of 'power/knowledge relations'. Drawing closely on Nietzsche (1968), Foucault (1977: 27) argues that 'power and knowledge directly imply one another . . . [such] that there is no power relation without the correlative constitution of a field of knowledge, nor any knowledge that does not presuppose and constitute at the same time power relations'. Thus he charts the way in which the discourses of the human sciences were intimately connected to the development and spread of disciplinary technologies in the modern period. He even goes as far as to suggest that the birth of the human sciences was 'probably to be found in . . . "ignoble" archives, where the modern play of coercion over bodies, gestures and behaviour has its beginnings' (Foucault 1977: 191).

Moreover, he shows how discourses shape material bodies and forms, though in this regard there is an important shift in emphasis. While in *Discipline and Punish* there is a 'filtering out of experience', such that power merely shapes and manipulates material bodies, in *The History of Sexuality* Foucault examines the way in which discourses on sexuality contribute to the constitution of human beings as subjects (McNay 1994: 104). In this perspective, the complexes of 'power/knowledge' are condensed, transmitted and resisted via historically constituted discourses. Retaining his archaeological commitment to develop a non-reductionist conception of discourse, but linking discourse to the whole gamut of non-discursive practices and political strategies surrounding sexuality, Foucault thus presents a new conception of discourse.

To capture the new conception, it is worth quoting the following passage at some length:

> What is said about sex must not be analyzed simply as the surface projection of . . . power mechanisms. *Indeed, it is in discourse that power and knowledge are joined together.* And for this very reason, we must conceive discourse as a series of discontinuous segments whose tactical function is neither uniform nor stable. To be more precise, we must not imagine a world of discourse divided between accepted discourse and excluded discourse, or between the dominant discourse and the dominated one; but as a multiplicity of discursive elements that can come into play in various strategies . . . Discourses are not once and for all subservient to power or raised up against it, any more than silences are. We must make allowance for the complex and unstable process whereby discourse can be both an instrument and an effect of power, but also a hindrance, a stumbling block, a point of resistance and a starting point for an opposing strategy. Discourse transmits and produces power; it reinforces it, but also undermines and exposes it, renders it fragile and makes it possible to thwart it.
>
> (Foucault 1979a: 100–1; emphasis added)

Understood in these terms, Foucault's (1980a: 194–8) new conception is more akin to what he calls a *dispositif* or an apparatus. Distinguishing this device from the earlier idea of an *episteme*, he stresses its role as a sort of 'grid of interpretation' that is shared both by the objects of Foucault's inquiries and by the researcher himself (Dreyfus and Rabinow 1982: 121).

Moreover, the grid comprises both discursive and non-discursive elements, as well as power and knowledge, all of which are contingently linked together by the apparatus itself. As Foucault (1980a: 194) puts it, a *dispositif* is 'a thoroughly heterogeneous ensemble consisting of discourses, institutions, architectural forms, regulatory decisions, laws, administrative reforms, scientific statements, philosophical, moral and philanthropic propositions – in short, the said as much as the unsaid'. The function of the *dispositif* is to enable the genealogist to account for the emergence of practices and institutions, and to place these elements in a broader and critical perspective. Thus, for instance, the repressive hypothesis might be regarded as a particular paradigm of meanings and behaviour, which can be contextualized and criticized when located within the broader logics of bio-power.

Foucault's substitution of power/knowledge configurations for discourses as systems of scientific statements marks an important shift towards incorporating non-discursive factors into the explanation of historical change. However, the new conception of discourse also marks a deliberate exclusion of the concept of ideology, which historically has represented one possible means of connecting discourses and material practices, and simultaneously making possible the critique of false beliefs (see Habermas 1978; Žižek 1989, 1994; Barrett 1991). Foucault (1980a: 118), opposes the notion of ideology for three reasons. In the first place, he argues that ideology 'always stands in virtual opposition to something else which is supposed to count as truth'. Thus, by drawing upon the 'framework relativist' theory of truth developed in the 'Order of Discourse', Foucault (1980a: 118) argues that the crucial distinction is not to be drawn at the level of true or false statements, 'but in seeing historically how effects of truth are produced within discourses which in themselves are neither true nor false'. Secondly, he argues that 'the concept of ideology refers ... to something of the order of a subject'. In other words, it presupposes a conception of human subjectivity that is either deceived by the operation of ideology, or able to break decisively with false beliefs and become enlightened. Finally, according to Foucault, 'ideology stands in a secondary position relative to something which functions as its infrastructure, as its material, economic determinant'.

Subject positions, bodies and subjectivization

What emerges from Foucault's alternative picture of discourse is the enmeshing of power, truth and practices, and the positioning of human beings within these historical configurations. Continuing in this vein, Foucault's (1982: 208) final writings recast his lifetime's work around the question of the subject. He argues that his 'object has been to create a history of the different modes by which, in our culture, human beings are made subjects'. He goes on to pinpoint three modes of 'objectification' by which human beings are transformed into subjects, and these logics are seen to parallel the overall development of his thought. The first involves the substitution of a linguistic for a philosophical conception of the subject. Thus, as is evident in his archaeological approach, Foucault (1982: 208) dispenses with the unified and constitutive philosophical subject of knowledge, *à la* Kant, Hegel and Husserl, and concentrates on what he calls the 'author-function' or 'the objectivization of the speaking subject'. In other words, he emphasizes the discursive conditions that make knowledge possible; thus subjects are little more than 'ways of speaking' within a particular discourse. This results in a certain 'decentring' of the subject – the (in)famous 'death of the author' – and a dispersion of the possible places from which one can speak.

The second logic of subject formation centres on what he calls the operation of 'dividing practices', in which the 'subject is either divided inside himself or divided from others'. Here Foucault is referring to the social and political processes by which divisions of 'self' and 'other' – for example, mad and sane, sick and healthy, criminals and 'good boys' – are produced in specific historical conjunctures. However, this formulation represents a reinterpretation of Foucault's (1980a: 186) earlier accounts of the way in which disciplinary technologies literally produce 'docile bodies' without the mediation of discourses, representations and consciousness, all of which are dismissed because of their humanistic connotations. This conception is modified in the first volume of *The History of Sexuality*, where he emphasizes the way in which human beings turn themselves into subjects via a series of confessional technologies. Nevertheless, he still concedes a primary explanatory role to relations of power and domination, as the 'obligation to confess is now relayed through so many different points, is so deeply ingrained in us, that we no longer perceive it as *the effect of a power that constrains us*' (Foucault 1979a: 60).

It is only in his third logic of subjectivization that Foucault (see 1985, 1990) focuses explicitly on the way in which human beings turn themselves into subjects through processes of recognition, self-mastery and transgression. Foucault (1991b: 11) is here interested 'in the way in which the subject constitutes himself in an active fashion, by the practices of the self'. However, while Foucault's 'ethics of the self' or an 'aesthetics of existence' places more emphasis on the practices human subjects engage in as agents, 'these practices are . . . not something that the individual invents by himself'. Rather, '[t]hey are patterns that he finds in his culture and which are proposed, suggested and imposed on him by his culture, his society and his social group' (Foucault 1991b: 11). In brief, it is only in his final writings that Foucault offers a conception of subjectivity that can mediate between the subordination of the subject to the all-pervasive logics of disciplinary power, and a constitutive concept of the subject 'decentred' by archaeological critique.

These final conceptions of the self and subjectivity give rise to Foucault's (1991b: 12) most suggestive account of the relationship between domination, discourse and freedom. The category of domination refers to relatively fixed systems of control, which strongly reduce the freedom of the subject, confining it to sedimented positions within a social structure. By contrast, the exercise of power presupposes a weakening of control, and the emergence of possibilities not evident in the existing structure of domination. This makes possible a certain degree of freedom for social agents both to maintain systems of domination and to propose counter-strategies of resistance. At this level of analysis, any struggle designed to modify existing social relations and to institute a new system of domination encounters resistance that has to be overcome. This assumes that any drive to create a new system of power will itself be an unstable configuration, always vulnerable to change and transformation.

Beyond Foucault?

The last two chapters have examined the vitally important contributions of Michel Foucault in developing a theory of discourse for social and political analysis. While there are divergences and difficulties in each of these different accounts, it is important to note in conclusion the common aspects of Foucault's approach, as well as some of the unresolved questions in his work.

1. At the outset, Foucault stresses the way discourses partly form social relations, identities and social objects. In this way, he emphasizes the materiality and positivity of discourse, which cannot be reduced to more primary processes, such as economic production, social institutions or political behaviour.

2. Foucault also makes possible a relational and historical conception of discourse. Especially in his later writings, he stresses the ever changing connections between different discourses, as well as the contingent relationships between discursive and non-discursive practices. In shifting his focus of attention from the analysis of

epistemes to *dispositifs*, which epitomizes the shift from his archaeological to his genealogical approach, Foucault seeks to incorporate non-discursive elements, such as institutions, policies and material objects, into a viable discursive approach to social and political phenomena.

3. Foucault consistently stresses that his main objects of inquiry are discursive *practices*. He thus captures the performative and practical aspects of speaking, writing and communicating, and connects them to questions of power, subjectivity and the body. Nevertheless, despite these innovations, Foucault never formalizes his conception of discourse in a satisfactory fashion. While concepts such as the *dispositif* enable one to conceive of connections between disparate discursive and non-discursive elements, the boundaries between different dispositifs, and their interconnection, are not properly explored.

4. Foucault endeavours at all stages of his writings to develop specific research tools and techniques to analyse discourses and their relationships with other discursive and non-discursive practices. In *The Archaeology of Knowledge*, Foucault sets out an entire 'panoply' of concepts and tools for the analysis of discourses, and in his genealogies of power, the body and sexuality, he introduces a crucial set of ideas to explain the emergence and formation of discourses and practices.

5. Hand in hand with these methodological tools and logics, Foucault also develops a set of philosophical reflections on questions of truth, method and knowledge, which make possible a theory of knowledge that underpins a discursive approach to social and political investigation. Moreover, these methodological and epistemological reflections, especially in the genealogical and problematizing modes, engender a particular way of combining descriptive and explanatory objectives with a critical ethos toward the objects of inquiry.

6. Foucault contributes a series of important substantive conclusions about modern society, as well as a crucial set of theoretical concepts and logics for its further investigation. Of particular importance in this regard are his suggestive thoughts about domination, power/resistance and political subjectivity. The great strength of Foucault's theorization of domination is his refusal to concede to a totalizing and all-encompassing power rooted in the overarching logics of commodification or rationalization, as do other 'critical theories'. Thus, in contrast to Weber's (1978)

sociology or Adorno and Horkheimer's *Dialectic of Enlightenment* (1973), Foucault does not present us with a total system of domination that imposes a rationalizing bureaucratic logic or class interest on a manipulated and deluded subaltern grouping. Foucault's objections to these accounts concentrate on the assumption that there is a 'true consciousness' or 'essence' that is being contaminated by power and domination – in other words, that there is a singular mechanism to which power relations are functional and can be made intelligible; that resistance to power and domination is negligible, and always integrated into the Moloch-like system of domination. In so doing, Foucault develops further the key distinction between domination and power, while articulating a productive notion of power that is not antithetical to freedom, subjectivity and resistance.

Remaining questions

Having said this, it is ironic that the major criticisms of Foucault's approach focus on his failure to give sufficient emphasis to the alternative spaces and counter-logics of resistance (see Poulantzas 1978: 77–80; Taylor 1985: 152–84; Habermas 1987b: 266–93; McNay 1994: 102–4; Dews 1995: 144–99). These criticisms fail for the most part to register Foucault's theoretical stress on the inextricability of power/resistance. They also posit an underlying ground for their conceptions of critique, which Foucault puts into question. Thus Dews, Habermas and McNay, and to a lesser extent Taylor, rely on a rational communicative action grounded on a universal reason, while Poulantzas depends on the unifying dynamics of the capitalist mode of production to dispute Foucault's claims.

However, their criticisms do make clear the lack of conceptual clarity in Foucault's account of power, and its relationship to the concepts of domination, resistance and the subject. These concern questions as to whether resistance is to be understood as either internal or external to the structure of domination and the play of power struggles, as well as our understanding of the emergence and articulation of resistances to systems of power/knowledge. They also point to the dearth of concrete analyses of resistance in Foucault's writings. In this sense, *Discipline and Punish* and certain sections of *The History of Sexuality* create the impression that disciplinary power and 'bio-power' are all-encompassing logics of objectification, rationalization and subjectivization, which exclude the possibility of resistance.

Another difficulty in Foucault's account is the relationship between the 'micro' and 'macro' levels of his analysis. As many commentators have suggested, while Foucault is correct to problematize a descending concept of power, in which the concrete deployments and strategies of power are the manifestations of some global logic, the precise linkage between the local and the global is not fully theorized. Thus, though Foucault's writings explore the 'micro-physics' of power/resistance, they do not adequately address the formation and dissolution of systems of domination. From this perspective, the relationship between the global question of domination and the more local power/resistance dialectic can only be clarified with a category like that of hegemony, that is, as systems of domination which are formed through power struggles that become sedimented over time.

We are thus confronted with four main difficulties in Foucault's conception of discourse. These are his failure to formalize satisfactorily his theory of discourse; his inadequate conceptualization of power/resistance; his lack of concrete analyses of resistances to power; and his inability (or refusal) to examine the 'macro' strategies and outcomes of power/resistance struggles. In Chapter 6 we will assess the extent to which these difficulties are accounted for by a post-Marxist conception of hegemony and subjectivity. More specifically, we will assess to what extent Laclau and Mouffe's concept of hegemony, which is founded on a particular theory of discourse, can account for the unification of the different sites of Foucault's 'micro-physics' of power/resistance so as to produce certain 'society effects'. Finally, we will assess the extent to which Laclau and Mouffe's distinction between 'subject position' and 'political subjectivity', and their introduction of a moment of identification and 'decision', provide a more adequate conception of subjectivity and political agency.

5

The Limits of Ideology in Marxist Theory

There are a number of reasons why it is important to examine the Marxist theory of ideology in the context of this book. To begin with, Marxism offers a distinctive account of the role of ideas, consciousness and language in politics and society. Not only does it relate ideas and representations to processes of economic production, but it also articulates a powerful theory of ideology in which beliefs are explained with reference to the uneven distribution of power and resources in class-divided societies. Two further reasons arise from the particular argument I am advancing. On the one hand, Marxists such as Louis Althusser and Michel Pêcheux have elaborated important conceptions of ideology and discourse that need to be evaluated in their own terms. On the other hand, the Marxist theory of ideology provides an essential backdrop to the emergence of Laclau and Mouffe's conception of discourse, which emerges from a deconstructive reading of the Marxist tradition. In order to explore these developments, I begin by outlining the classical Marxist concept of ideology, after which I examine the ways in which Antonio Gramsci, Althusser and Pêcheux attempt to resolve some of the difficulties of the original approach.

Classical Marxism

Simplifying considerably, Marxism is concerned with the way in which human beings interact with nature to produce and reproduce their material conditions of existence. It emphasizes how social and political questions can be explained by understanding the ways in which material production is socially organized. As Marx (1977a: 389) puts it, 'legal relations' and 'forms of the state . . . have their roots in the material conditions of life', and their 'anatomy . . . is to be sought in political economy'. This gives rise to the famous 'base/superstructure' model of society, in which political and ideological phenomena are understood in terms of economic relations and logics. More specifically, Marx purports to discover the contradictory and crisis-ridden character of material production in class-divided societies. As against theories of social life that emphasize order, consensus and stability, Marx emphasizes the contradiction between the relations and forces of production, and the contradiction between opposed social classes, which are defined by their ownership or non-ownership of the means of production. The first serves as 'the guiding thread of his studies' and the key principle of historical analysis. In capitalist society it turns on the tension between, on the one hand, the tendency towards the unfettered expansion of technology and labour power, and on the other the private ownership of the means of production, which impedes the full development of the productive forces. The second contradiction concerns the struggle between social classes, which Marx and Engels (1985) argue is the key political logic of history. In capitalist societies it is the conflict between the bourgeoisie and the proletariat that constitutes its central political dynamic.

The combined impact of these two contradictory sets of processes is the crisis and eventual downfall of capitalism, and its replacement by a new, more rational mode of production structured around the common ownership of the means of production (Marx 1992). How this is to be accomplished, and the obstacles to its achievement, bring us to Marx's political theory. As the most dominated class in capitalist society, the proleteriat has to overthrow the capitalist state and construct a new society in its own image. It must transform itself from what Marx and Engels (1985) call a 'class-in-itself' into a 'class-for-itself', thus attaining consciousness of itself as an exploited and dominated group. This entails the elaboration of a revolutionary ideology and the creation of an organizational infrastructure, by which to envisage and attain emancipation from capitalist rule. By contrast, the bourgeoisie sustains its rule through a combination of force and ideological conditioning. Hence the modern liberal democratic state is seen as the major institutional means of 'managing the common affairs of the whole bourgeoisie', while 'political power . . .

is ... merely the organised power of one class for oppressing another' (Marx and Engels 1985: 82, 105). In short, political questions in classical Marxism concern the role of the state and ideology (the 'superstructures') in maintaining class domination, in which the state is understood principally as an agent of coercion, and ideology as the inculcation of 'false consciousness'.

Although Marx and Engels (1970: 53; Marx 1977b) supplement this bold expression of their theory with more complex arguments when they analyse particular events and historical situations, it is their conception of ideology that concerns us here. Marx deploys the concept of ideology in at least three ways. On one level, it is used to attack philosophical theories which claim that 'the world is ruled by ideas, that ideas and concepts are the determining principles' (quoted in Wood 1981: 117). On another level, Marx uses the concept of ideology to explain how ideas and 'forms of consciousness' legitimize and 'naturalize' certain forms of social arrangement (such as the ownership of private property), or represent and enhance certain class interests. In this sense, the concept functions as a tool of analysis that enables Marx to examine the ways in which beliefs enable certain sets of social relations to be reproduced and maintained. Finally, Marx argues that ideology not only contributes to the reproduction of social life, but also involves a form of 'false consciousness' or systematic illusion, in which ideological beliefs are not just incorrect, but render one ignorant of the 'real motive forces' of thought, which are always to be found in the material conditions of life (Morrice 1996: 36). These ideological distortions or 'inverted representations' are rooted in a social world that is itself inverted and contradictory. For instance, in his famous discussion of 'commodity fetishism', Marx (1992) argues that the value of commodities in capitalist societies appears as intrinsic to the commodities themselves – their price or desirability in the market-place – whereas value is always produced by human labour power. Our worshipping of commodities such as motor cars and mobile telephones thus conceals the true nature of economic production in capitalism, and conjures up an ideological illusion.

While there are heated debates about the precise status and plausibility of Marx and Engels's arguments (cf. Plamenatz 1970; Larrain 1979; Barrett 1991; Hall 1996), there is some consensus that their theory of ideology is largely negative, reductionist and in varying degrees deterministic. It is negative in the sense that it is largely critical of ideology believing it to mystify and deceive people about their true interests and sources of belief. This conception can be differentiated from more positive or at least neutral accounts of ideology, which accept that ideologies are an integral part of all societies and not just illusory sets of ideas and beliefs. It is reductionist in that it understands and explains ideologies by relating them to more important social processes, such as the ways human beings organize their economic production. Hence Marx and Engels (1970: 64) view ideas and 'forms of consciousness' as expressions of particular class interests. Finally, Marx and Engels are accused of being economic determinists in that they explain the genesis and transformation of ideologies in terms of the changes in the economic structure of society. As Marx (1977a: 389) puts it in a famous statement of his materialist theory, social change cannot be judged by its 'own consciousness'; instead, 'consciousness must be explained ... from the contradictions of material life, from the existing conflict between the social productive forces and the relations of production'.

Marx's extraordinarily rich reflections on the concept of ideology thus bequeath an ambiguous legacy. On the one hand, he links ideas, consciousness and discourse to ongoing social and political processes, thus breaking with idealist approaches to language and social meaning, which focus too narrowly on concepts and ideas abstracted from social relations. On the other hand, he tends to view ideologies and discourses as secondary to more essential phenomena, such as the laws of economic development and class conflict, thus neglecting their own autonomy and materiality. It has been left to later Marxists such as Gramsci, Althusser and Pêcheux, as well as those working within the Frankfurt School such as Jürgen Habermas, to provide a more positive conception of ideology and discourse, which does not reduce it to more determinant social processes, but which retains a critical edge.

Gramsci

The Italian Marxist, Antonio Gramsci (1971: 162), endeavours to break with economistic and reductionist interpretations of the 'base/superstructure' model of society by emphasizing the role of 'the ideological forms' in which 'men become conscious of conflicts in the world of the economy' and fight them out. In so doing, Gramsci rejects the view that ideologies are merely systems of 'false consciousness' or mistaken belief. This conception results from a crucial ambiguity in the Marxist conception of ideology, in which it is both a necessary aspect of any particular social order and a negative term designed to criticize consciousness that is divorced from social reality. Instead, he distinguishes between the idea of 'historically organic ideologies' and 'Ideology' as a pure realm of disembodied ideas, which simply reflects the underlying determinants of society, or the intentions of individual thinkers. Historically organic ideologies are 'necessary to a given structure', as they represent the material interests of a class and are thus organically related to the social institutions of society as a whole. By contrast, 'Ideology' as a pure realm of disembodied ideas is an 'arbitrary, rationalistic, or "willed"' construction that is reducible to the material and physiological sensations of individuals (Gramsci 1971: 376–7).

In privileging the organic conception of ideology, Gramsci develops a more positive or neutral conception of ideology over Marx's essentially negative or critical usage. Ideologies thus 'have a validity which is psychological; they "organise" human masses, and create the terrain on which men move, acquire consciousness of their position, struggle, etc.', and in practice they 'assume the fanatical granite compactness of ... "popular beliefs"', and manifest 'the same energy as "material forces"' (Gramsci 1971: 377). In short, successfully articulated ideologies for Gramsci (1971: 328) are commonsensical conceptions of the world, which are 'implicitly manifest in art, law, in economic activity and in all manifestations of individual and collective life', rather than imaginary mental representations utterly divorced from social practices.

Gramsci's reworking of the Marxist concept of ideology goes hand in hand with his new conception of hegemony. This is a central concept for Gramsci because it unifies his different ideas and logics into a coherent theoretical approach. In brief, he seeks to provide a novel account of class rule in capitalist society that does not rely simply on the coercive power of the state and the instilling of 'false consciousness' by the bourgeoisie. Building on his more positive conception of ideology, he stresses that in addition to the use of force and ideological deception, ruling groups in society need to win the consent of those they govern, and winning the consent of those subordinated to its power means that a ruling class must establish its authority and legitimacy in society as a whole, and not just by virtue of its economic position or by control over the government and the state. Gramsci thus places great stress on understanding the different types of relationship between rulers and ruled, and he distinguishes between active and passive consent, as well as between organic and inorganic forms of rule (see Femia 1981: 23–60). He also emphasizes the important role of culture and consciousness in determining questions of politics and strategy. This leads him to conclude that consent is mainly manufactured and exercised in 'civil society', which consists of 'private' associations and institutions, such as schools, churches, the family, as well as the realm of culture more generally, as opposed to 'political society' or 'the state' narrowly construed. In Gramsci's (1971: 161, 180–5) terms, therefore, a ruling class must achieve 'intellectual and moral leadership', and not just 'political leadership', if it is to govern effectively and efficiently.

This reconceptualization of the nature and dynamics of class rule leads Gramsci to develop a new political strategy for subordinate classes such as the proleteriat. As against Lenin's strategy of constructing temporary alliances between distinct classes – workers, middle classes and peasants – in a bid to overthrow class rule, he argues that social classes must transcend their narrow economic interests and elaborate a new ideology. Gramsci (1971: 125–33) stresses that these different classes and groups must come to share a common set of political objectives, based on a new set of beliefs and practices, by forging a new 'collective will'. In other words, politics ceases to be a zero-sum game conducted by classes with fixed identities and interests, and becomes more a process of constructing relationships and agreements amongst divergent groups and classes. Moreover, it occurs largely in the realm of civil society and consists of 'winning over' agents and groups to certain ideological and political positions. Gramsci calls this strategy of winning hegemony in civil society before the attainment of state power a 'war of position', and he distinguishes this approach from a 'war of movement' or 'war of manoeuvre' in which the aim of politics is a direct and rapid confrontation between opposed forces.

Gramsci's development of the concept of hegemony results in a general reorientation of Marxist political theory. Most importantly, he proposes a new topography of social relations in Marxist theory by expanding the category of 'political society' (or the state) to include 'private' associations and activities, which Hegel had bracketed under the name of civil society. He also transforms the functions of class domination to encompass the manufacture of consent, and the exercise of 'leadership' through 'ethico-political' and 'intellectual and moral' means, especially within the realm of civil society.

Both of these developments were predicated on a sharp separation between Eastern and Western Europe, in which Gramsci (1971: 238) distinguishes between 'the East', where 'the State was everything, [and] civil society was primordial and gelatinous', and the West, where 'there was a proper balance between State and civil society'. This meant that in the more complex and organized countries of the West there ought to be a prioritization of the 'war of position' over the 'war of movement' as the most appropriate political strategy for advancing socialism by the working classes.

In short, as Norberto Bobbio (1988) notes perceptively, Gramsci engineers a twofold inversion of the Marxist base/superstructure model of society. Whereas Marx privileges the primacy of economic production, focusing his attention on the contradictory relationship between the forces and relations of production, Gramsci emphasizes the ideological superstructures ('state plus civil society') over the economic structure. In addition, within the realm of the superstructures, Gramsci asserts the priority of civil society (the moment of consent and consensus) over political society (the moment of force or coercion). However, while Bobbio correctly pinpoints the principal elements of Gramsci's contribution to Marxist political theory, the idea of a simple reversal of the classical oppositions crucially misses Gramsci's endeavours to reconnect the dualisms he introduces (Gramsci 1971: 169–70; see also Texier 1979). For instance, while Gramsci rethinks the relationship between state and civil society in Marxist theory, he also introduces the idea of the 'integral state' to account for both the hegemonic and dictatorial aspects of political rule. This leads to a general redefinition of the Marxist theory of the state. Rather than just an instrument of class rule, Gramsci (1971: 244) identifies it with 'the entire complex of practical and theoretical activities with which the ruling class not only justifies and maintains its dominance, but manages to win the active consent of those over whom it rules'. Similarly, the concept of a 'historical bloc' articulates both structural and superstructural elements of society – the 'decisive economic nucleus', political society and civil society – as a 'unity of opposites and distincts' (Gramsci 1971: 137). Historical blocs are thus configurations of related elements, although they are ultimately organized around a fundamental social class and a dominant mode of production.

Gramsci's path-breaking contributions to Marxist theory have opened up a number of fruitful avenues of investigation. In particular, his new conceptions of ideology and hegemony, as well as his stress on the role of political agents in bringing about social change, reinvigorated the Marxist theory of politics and ideology. One important development engendered in part by Gramsci's writings was the structuralist Marxism of Louis Althusser and his school, and it is to this influential approach that I shall now turn.

Althusser and Pêcheux

Emanating from an epistemological and sociological critique of humanistic and reductionist Marxism, the Althusserian conception of ideology and society represents a major reworking of Marxist social and political theory. On an epistemological level, Althusser defends what he calls Marxist science against 'theoretical humanism'. He argues that Marx's scientific account of history and society only emerged in his later writings, especially in *Capital*, while his earlier writings were under the sway of idealist philosophers such as Hegel and Ludwig Feuerbach. His argument is based on the idea that every genuine science breaks with a pre-scientific ideological past by producing its own theoretical object of investigation around which intellectual labour can be organized (Althusser 1969: 35–7, 46–7; Althusser and Balibar 1970: 30, 44–5).

On a sociological level, Althusser (1969: 221–31) claims that ideology does not comprise an abstract set of ideas divorced from the social world, nor does it simply reflect an already existing reality. These models suggest that ideology is concerned with the way in which social actors or subjects experience the world of objects in a distorted form, or impose illusory mental constructions on social reality. This 'false consciousness' model of ideology presupposes either an empiricist or naive realist epistemology, in which subjects are seen to represent or misrepresent an external social reality, or a form of idealism in which the world simply consists of ideas or representations. Instead, Althusser (1971) argues that ideology is vital for the reproduction of society and produces real material effects. According to Althusser, ideology must be viewed as a social 'practice' whose function is to turn individuals into subjects. It provides subjects with particular characteristics, such as a 'class outlook' and a specific social and political identity. These 'class outlooks' are embodied in the social institutions and rituals that underpin beliefs and forms of consciousness. For instance, Althusser discusses the way in which believers in the Catholic faith come to 'live out' their particular religious beliefs and identity. This 'living out' of religious beliefs includes a set of practices, rituals and performances (confession, praying, participating in mass) within historically specific institutions (the Roman Catholic Church, with its particular organization and hierarchy).

Althusser's twofold theoretical battle against theoretical human-ism and reductionism is united in his theory of ideology. On the one hand, science can only constitute itself as science by distinguishing itself from ideological discourse, which remains oblivious to its own humanistic, idealist and essentialist assumptions. On the other hand, ideology as a 'lived relation' between social subjects in society is connected to questions of truth and falsity, and by exten-sion to epistemological problems. This connection arises from the particular function of ideological practices, which is to ensure the smooth reproduction of the inherently unstable and contradictory nature of class societies. This can only be achieved, for Althusser (1969: 233), because ideology is an 'imaginary', albeit 'lived', relation that a subject has to its real conditions of existence. In other words, the function of ideology is to make the world in which the subject lives appear obvious and natural, even though this apparent objectivity and normality is an effect of the subject 'mis-recognizing' its real historical situation. For example, workers in liberal capitalist societies may perceive themselves to be free agents with equal citizenship rights. However, this 'lived relation' system-atically causes subjects to 'misrecognize' the way in which their labour power is being exploited in market societies, thus facilitating the reproduction of capitalist relations of production.

Althusser's understanding of the role and function of ideology in Marxism entails a fundamental restructuring of the Marxist con-ception of society. Drawing on structuralist theory, he argues that social formations comprise three systems or levels of practice (economic, political and ideological), each of which has its own 'relative autonomy' in sustaining a particular society. Any society is thus a complex articulation of elements in which one of the levels plays the dominant role and social contradictions are to be under-stood as complex and 'overdetermined' phenomena, which are not reducible to economic processes alone. In this conception, import-ant social change occurs when multiple contradictions are fused together or condensed into a revolutionary rupture (Althusser 1969: 89–116). Ultimately, however, it is the economic system that determines which level is going to be dominant in a particular society. For instance, he argues that in feudal societies ideological practices such as those sustained by the Christian church were dominant, although this role was allocated by economic practices, and economic practices were 'in the final instance' the determining factors that shaped feudal life.

In his later writings, Althusser introduces an important distinction between the repressive state apparatuses and the ideological state apparatuses in order to stress the importance of ideological and subjective factors in reproducing capitalist societies. These sets of institutions are roughly equivalent to Gramsci's categories of political and civil society. Thus repressive state apparatuses such as the army, police and legal system function 'by violence', whereas ideological state apparatuses such as schools, religious institutions, the family, the media and political associations function 'by ideology'. This gives further substance to Althusser's argument that ideological beliefs are not just free-floating ideas generated by human beings, but are 'materialized' in specific types of institutions and organizations. For instance, it is within the organization and functioning of institutions such as schools that ideas such as 'competition', 'individualism' and 'discipline' take on a material form and become embodied in particular practices and actions.

In addition to developing a new conception of ideology and society in Marxist theory, Althusser is also concerned to develop a novel theory of subjectivity. Borrowing from structuralist and psychoanalytical theory, especially Lacan's interpretation of Freud, he shows how the human subject is an ideological effect rather than a self-constituting thing or agent. He argues that in order for a subject to acquire an identity, it must 'freely' subject itself to a 'Subject', such as God in religious ideology, which in turn enables the subject to 'centre' itself and recognize other subjects as subjects. This process of acquiring a stable identity both for itself and others provides the subject 'with the absolute guarantee that everything really is so' and that 'everything will be all right' (Althusser 1971: 181). Althusser (1971: 174) introduces the mechanism of interpellation to capture the process by which a subject both recognizes and misrecognizes itself as a subject:

> [I]deology 'acts' or 'functions' in such a way that it 'recruits' among the individuals (it recruits them all) by that very precise operation which I have called *interpellation* or hailing, and which can be imagined along the lines of the most commonplace everyday police (or other) hailing: 'Hey, you there!'
>
> Assuming that the theoretical scene I have imagined takes place in

the street, the hailed individual will turn around. By this one-hundred-and-eighty-degree physical conversion, he becomes a *subject*. Why? Because he has recognized that the hail was 'really' addressed to him (and not someone else).

This conception has its roots in Lacan's (1977: 1–7) famous discussion of 'the mirror-stage' in which the 'helpless' human infant literally recognizes itself in an external mirror image, thereby entering the symbolic order of meaning and signification. Interpellation is thus a 'speculary' or mirror-like process, in which a subject can only recognize itself in an external image that is fixed and absolute, and it is this fixed image which can in turn confer an identity on the subject. For example, in the United Kingdom it is in the figure of the Queen (or King) that British people literally recognize themselves as 'political subjects' or 'subjects of the Crown', and not free and equal citizens (see Nairn 1990).

An immediate difficulty with Althusser's theory of the subject is his emphasis on the way in which social structures determine the positioning of subjects *before* they are interpellated (Hirst 1979: 64–8). This confines his theory of subjectivity to processes of recognition and misrecognition, which tends to presume the idea of a unified subject that can be centred by the imaginary relation conferred to it in the 'hailing' process. Michel Pêcheux (1982) attempts to address this tension in the Althusserian framework by drawing more systematically on Saussure's structural linguistics and the psychoanalytical insights of Freud and Lacan. He insists that the subject does not just recognize and misrecognize itself in an interpellation. Rather an individual brings itself into existence by *identifying* with an external object (Pêcheux 1982: 79). In this way, Pêcheux emphasizes Lacan's radical claim that the subject literally constitutes itself as a subject by identifying with the mirror image. Just as the character in Woody Allen's film *Play it Again, Sam* can only become a viable human agent when he identifies with the film-star Humphrey Bogart, so human beings identify with an external object, image or ideology to give sense and meaning to their lives (see Žižek 1989: 109–10).

To explain this effect Pêcheux introduces the mechanisms of preconstruction and articulation, both of which depend on his concept of a discursive formation. The concept of preconstruction captures the way in which the subject's identification with something external is concealed within discourse by appearing to be its own ground or cause. This is what Pêcheux (1982: 108) calls the 'Munchausen effect' – 'in memory of the immortal Baron who *lifted himself in the air by pulling up his own hair*' – in which the subject appears self-evidently and obviously to be a unified and sovereign entity. For instance, in bourgeois ideology the myth of the 'self-made man' pulling himself up by his own bootstraps conceals the structural preconditions for capital accumulation by suggesting that hard work, self-sacrifice and genius are the necessary and sufficient conditions for entrepreneurial success.

To account for this, Pêcheux introduces a radical conception of language in which meaning is an effect of interpellation. Hence Pêcheux refuses any separation between the theory of meaning (semantics) and the way subjects are formed by ideological practices. This suggests that there is no significant distinction between meaning and the particular discourse within which it is produced. In short, meaning is produced at the same time as individuals are interpellated as subjects, that is, when they come to recognize themselves as subjects with specific experiences and understandings of the world. Pêcheux draws attention to another mechanism, articulation, that gives the subject the illusion that it 'causes itself' within discourse (or what Pêcheux calls the 'inter-discourse'). This mechanism refers to the way in which the subject strives to order meaning within a particular discourse. For instance, it captures the way in which a subject accounts for incidents in its life by weaving together contingent events and accidents into a seamless whole, thus enabling it (and its audience) to draw the 'correct' implications and inferences from the discursive articulation. This has the effect of providing coherence to discourse by making things follow on from one another so that external identifications are experienced as something already thought or said by the subject. Events and decisions are thus made to appear natural, normal and justified.

Pêcheux's work represents the most elaborate attempt to use Althusser's theory of ideology to develop an empirically applicable approach to discourse analysis. Not only does he locate the construction and functioning of discourses within the realm of ideological practices, he also develops methodological tools to conduct social and political analysis (Pêcheux *et al.* 1978). He also develops a contextual theory of meaning that breaks with the view that words or expressions simply represent or denote objects in the world, and prioritizes the symbolic dimension of all social meaning. Thus Pêcheux (1982: 189) argues that 'meaning does not exist anywhere except in the metaphorical relationships (realised in substitution effects, paraphrases, synonym formations) which happen to be more or less provisionally located historically in a given discursive formation'. This means that he can examine the interpellations and identifications of individuals as subjects purely at the level of language – what he calls, following Lacan, 'the primacy of the signifier' – and without recourse to an essentialist theory of society or human beings.

Nevertheless, despite Pêcheux's best efforts to provide a defensible approach to the study of ideology and discourse, he cannot free himself from the straitjacket of structural Marxism. His approach remains entrapped within Saussure's privileging of *langue* as a static and unconscious system of linguistic differences, and this militates against a historical and contingent conception of meaning and signification. He also accepts Saussure's binary distinction between signifiers and signifieds, which Derrida has carefully problematized. Most importantly, he is unable to overcome the problems underpinning the overall Althusserian theory of society and politics. In other words, although he stresses the role of discursive formations in determining meaning and constructing subjectivity, discourses are always located in the more determinate realm of ideological practices, and the ideological level forms one 'region' of the Althusserian 'structure-in-dominance'. It is, finally, to the Althusserian model of society that we must turn.

There is no question that Althusser's theoretical approach reinvigorated the Marxist theory of ideology and subjectivity. His stress on the relative autonomy of the three systems of practice that constitute a social formation, and his emphasis on the 'overdetermined' character of social contradictions, carried the promise of breaking with the reductionist and determinist model of society epitomized in the base/superstructure metaphor. However, his model is strongly compromised by his insistence that it is the economic system that determines which level is to be the dominant element in any particular society, and it is economic processes that still determine 'in the last instance' the functioning and reproduction of society as a whole. It is evident that this conception fails to transcend the determinism of the Marxist theory of society, in which case the 'relative autonomy' of the ideological and political superstructures is confined to providing the conditions for the overall reproduction of capitalist social relations.

Moreover, Althusser never fully spells out the initial grounds for separating the different levels of the social formation, nor does he

justify the fact that the economic and ideological levels perform
determining roles in all societies (Cutler *et al.* 1977: 207–21). The
major consequence of the separation of society into distinct
'regions' or 'levels' is to militate against a relational conception of
different systems of social practice. This idea is implicit in
Althusser's use of the Freudian concept of overdetermination in
which it is impossible to disentangle the different elements of
society as they are mutually imbricated. A final difficulty with the
Althusserian system of society is that there appears to be very little
space for conflicting forms of interpellation and identification,
which may challenge the existing 'structure-in-dominance'. This
confirms the functionalist overtones of the overall theoretical
model, in which each element has the purpose of maintaining the
reproduction of the system as a whole (Benton 1984: 105–7).

Deconstructing Marxism

My brief genealogy of the Marxist theory of ideology has pinpointed an important set of developments. I began by noting the
way in which the classical Marxist conception of ideology linked the
role of ideas and consciousness to the contradictory dynamics of
class-divided societies. I then showed how Gramsci, Althusser and
Pêcheux endeavoured to deal with the difficulties of the classical
model's tendency to reduce ideology to more determinate processes such as economic production and class struggle. Gramsci's
more positive conception of ideology, when allied to his new theory
of hegemony, made possible a different model of society in which
economic processes and class struggles were no longer the only
important elements. The Althusserian school extended these ideas
by stressing that society comprises three relatively autonomous systems of social practices, in which ideological practices perform the
crucial role of turning individuals into subjects with particular sorts
of identities and propensities. Finally, Michel Pêcheux has put forward an innovative conception of discourse to account for the
different mechanisms by which subjects constitute their identities in
certain ways.

Despite the fact that these writings have contributed enormously
to a coherent and empirically applicable theory of discourse, they
are all constrained by the underlying philosophical and methodological assumptions of Marxism. Put succinctly, these assumptions
suggest a fundamental dualism in Marxist theory between the more

important material logics of economic production and reproduction, on the one hand, and the less important ideological and political processes on the other. Thus, while the former set of processes forms a legitimate object of research and can be explained objectively and scientifically, the latter are either reflections of underlying economic logics or contingent and accidental phenomena, which are not governed by the more essential logics that determine social and historical change.

In short, the Marxist tradition is organized around a sharp binary opposition, which in Derridean terms is in need of deconstruction (cf. Anderson 1983: 34). According to Laclau and Mouffe (1985), this binary opposition is a product of the insurmountable tension in Marxist theory between the 'logic of necessity' and the 'logic of contingency'. We can trace this opposition with respect to the different Marxist contributions we have thus far examined. In the writings of Marx and Engels, the logics can be traced back to two competing theories of historical change. The first is epitomized in the '1859 Preface to *The Contribution to Political Economy*' where social change is determined by the contradiction between the forces and relations of production. The other is manifest in *The Communist Manifesto*, in which Marx and Engels stress the primacy of class struggles in the production of historical transformation (Laclau 1990: 5–15). Moreover, while both logics are present in Marxist theory they do not have an equal status. Rather than a conceptual connection between the two logics, Marxists posit a sharp separation between them, and prioritize the logic of necessity (see Derrida 1976: 141–64). Hence the logic of contingency, which is synonymous with intrinsically political questions such as subjectivity, strategy, the state and ideology, is systematically neglected. It is restricted to those aspects of society that cannot be rigorously explained in scientific terms, and is ultimately reduced to the necessary laws of economic development (Laclau and Mouffe 1985: 47–8).

This general problem is also evident in the Gramscian and Althusserian accounts of ideology and politics. In the case of Gramsci, it is possible to discern two essentialist and reductionist assumptions underpinning his reworking of Marxist theory. These are his commitment to a fundamental social class – the proletariat in capitalist societies – bringing about significant social change, and the centrality of a 'decisive economic nucleus' as both the main object of political struggle and the ultimate determinant of the character of the political and ideological superstructures. Both of these assumptions require the Marxist notions of a 'closed' conception of society with a set of predetermined laws of operation and development. From this perspective, Gramsci's innovative concept of hegemony, and his introduction of ideas such as the 'historical bloc' as a means of linking together different components of society in a non-reductive way, are compromised by an essentialist and linear theory of history (Laclau and Mouffe 1985: 65–71).

One encounters a similar clash between the logics of necessity and contingency in the Althusserian account of society and ideology. Both Althusser and Pêcheux attempt to develop a non-reductionist and anti-essentialist conception of society in which different levels have their own 'relative autonomy' and contradictions are complex and overdetermined.Nevertheless, they assert that economic practices ultimately determine the configurations and dynamics of social formations, and they retain a rigid a priori division of society into three distinct levels or regions of practice. Moreover, while both stress the 'material' character of ideology and the production of subjectivity, they remain wedded to the idea that the subject 'misrecognizes' its own real situation. This is predicated on a sharp and unwarranted split between science and ideology, in which Marxist theory *qua* science is granted an epistemological privilege in deciding what is 'false consciousness' and 'true consciousness'.

To conclude, post-Marxists such as Laclau and Mouffe challenge the Marxist conception of society and the theory of ideology it has spawned. They thus reject the idea that society can be separated into different types of practice on a priori grounds, as well as the idea that economic logics determine political and discursive processes. Instead, drawing upon and radicalizing post-structuralist concepts developed by Derrida, Foucault and Lacan, they replace the Marxist theory of ideology with a new conception of discourse. They argue that all practices are discursive and that no system of practice is completely immune from the effects of others, which means that ultimate determinacy is impossible. This is predicated on a new theory of articulatory practice, to which I shall turn in the next chapter.

6

Laclau and Mouffe's Theory of Discourse

The previous chapter concluded by pinpointing an inherent tension between the logics of necessity and contingency in the Marxist conception of ideology and society. In this chapter I continue this deconstructive reading of Marxism by examining Ernesto Laclau and Chantal Mouffe's conception of discourse, which is widely accepted by both sympathizers and sceptics alike as exemplifying the post-Marxist approach to discourse theory. They draw critically upon structuralist, post-structuralist and Marxist traditions of thinking in order to extend dramatically the scope of discourse theory to embrace all social practices and relations. Hence they do not restrict the scope of discourse analysis to purely linguistic phenomena, but regard them as 'worlds' of related objects and practices that form the identities of social actors. Their resultant conception of society strives to overcome the determinism and reductionism of Marxism, and develop an alternative research programme. I begin by outlining the main contours of Laclau and Mouffe's approach, which is built upon the related concepts of discourse and articulation.

Discourse

In its most general sense, the concept of discourse in Laclau and Mouffe's theory captures the idea that all objects and actions are meaningful, and that their meaning is conferred by particular systems of significant differences. Consider, for instance, a forest standing in the path of a proposed motorway. It may simply represent an inconvenient obstacle impeding the rapid implementation of a new road system, or it might be viewed as a site of special interest for scientists and naturalists, or a symbol of the nation's threatened natural heritage. In short, the meaning or 'being' of the forest – what it literally is for us – depends on the particular systems of difference or discourses that constitute its identity. In discourses of economic modernization, trees may be understood as the disposable means for continued economic growth or, in this example, as temporary obstacles to the rapid building of the motorway. In environmentalist discourses, by contrast, a forest might represent a viable ecosystem or an object of intrinsic value and beauty. Each of these discursive structures is a social and political construction, which establishes a system of relations between different objects and practices, while providing 'subject positions' with which social agents can identify. In our example, these subjects might be 'developers', 'naturalists', 'environmentalists' or 'eco-warriors'. In broader social and political terms, 'hegemonic projects' will attempt to weave together different strands of discourse in an effort to dominate or structure a field of meaning, thus fixing the identities of objects and practices in a particular way.

In order to explicate this theory of discourse, especially the idea of a discursive structure, we need to begin with the concept of an *articulatory practice*. Laclau and Mouffe (1985: 113) characterize the practice of articulation as '*the construction of nodal points which partially fix meaning*'. This fixation of meaning is always partial because of what they call '*the openness of the social*', which in turn is a consequence of the '*constant overflowing of every discourse by the infinitude of the field of discursivity*' (Laclau and Mouffe 1985: 113). To unpack these dense formulations, we need, firstly, to consider what they mean by discourse. Drawing on Foucault's archaeological writings, they argue that discursive formations consist of related elements that can 'in certain contexts of exteriority . . . be signified as a totality' (Laclau and Mouffe 1985: 106). They thus create an analogy between linguistic and social systems, as in both systems all identities are relational and all relations have a necessary character (see Benveniste 1971; Saussure 1974).

However, Laclau and Mouffe differ from the linguistic model in two important respects. First, systems of social relations are not purely linguistic phenomena, as 'a discursive structure is an articulatory practice which constitutes and organizes social relations' and not 'a merely "cognitive" or "contemplative" entity' (Laclau and Mouffe 1985: 96). For example, the ideas, policies and actions of Thatcherism can be seen as a discourse. Not only did it consist of a set of ideas ('freedom', 'monetarism', 'law and order'), it also inculcated a certain set of practices ('strong leadership', 'entrepreneurship'), and involved attempts to transform institutions and organizations, such as the British Conservative Party and the British state. Second, and most importantly, Laclau and Mouffe challenge the 'closure' of the linguistic model, which reduces all *elements* to the internal *moments* of a system. This implies that every social action simply repeats an already existing system of meanings and practices, in which case there is no possibility of constructing new 'nodal points' that 'partially fix meaning', which is the chief characteristic of an articulatory practice.

Instead, drawing upon post-structuralist conceptions of language, Laclau and Mouffe distinguish between 'contingent elements' in a discursive field and 'necessary moments' articulated into a particular discourse. Whereas particular discourses are partial fixations of social meaning, discursive fields are characterized by a 'surplus of meaning' that can never be fully exhausted by any specific discourse. That is to say, while discourses endeavour to impose order and necessity on a field of meaning, the ultimate contingency of meaning precludes this possibility from being actualized. Moreover, as discourses are relational entities whose identities depend on their differentiation from other discourses, they are themselves dependent and vulnerable to those meanings that are necessarily excluded in any discursive articulation. This is what Laclau and Mouffe (1985: 110–11) call a 'discursive exterior' and it means that the necessary moments of a discourse are also penetrated by contingency.

Extrapolating from this logic, Laclau and Mouffe claim that society itself can never be 'closed', as it is strictly an 'impossible object' of analysis. Instead, any society is 'overflowed' by a surplus of meaning, which makes up 'the social'. Returning to my earlier example of Thatcherism, their argument is not consonant with Mrs Thatcher's infamous claim that 'there is no such thing as society'. Rather, it points to the fact that, no matter how successful a particular political project's discourse might be in dominating a discursive field, it can never in principle completely articulate all elements, as there will always be forces against which it is defined. In fact, as we shall see, a discourse always requires a discursive 'outside' to constitute itself.

A final aspect of Laclau and Mouffe's account of discourse is their deconstruction of the distinction between discursive and non-discursive practices. Criticizing Foucault's ambiguous retention of this dichotomy, Laclau and Mouffe (1985: 107) argue that all objects are constituted as objects of discourse, and that there is no ontological difference between 'the linguistic and behavioural aspects of a social practice'. For instance, as speech-act theorists such as Austin (1975) have argued, saying something such as 'I do' in a wedding ceremony is just as much an action as exchanging the wedding rings. Both actions can only be understood as part of the wider meaningful practice of 'getting married'.

Laclau and Mouffe add two important qualifications in this regard. First, they do not contest the fact that objects have a 'real existence' outside discourse. What they deny is that objects have 'extra-discursive' *meaning*, and it is meaning that plays a central role in their approach. Second, they affirm the material, rather than mental, character of discourse. They thus blur the sharp separation between an objective world, on the one hand, and language or thought on the other, in which the latter is simply a representation or expression of the former. Discourses are not confined to an 'inner' realm of mental phenomena, but are those publicly available and essentially incomplete frameworks of meaning which enable social life to be conducted.

The primacy of politics

The 'open texturedness' of any discourse and the consequent contingency of all social identity leaves Laclau and Mouffe with a potential paradox. If all identity is relational and differential, and no discourse can in principle be closed, how is any identity or any society possible? Does their theory of discourse condemn us to a total free-play of meaning? Laclau and Mouffe tackle this paradox by affirming the primacy of politics in their social ontology. Systems of social relations, which are understood as articulated sets of discourses, are always political constructions involving the construction of antagonisms and the exercise of power. Moreover, because social systems have a fundamentally political character, they are rendered vulnerable to those forces that are excluded in the process of political constitution. It is around this set of processes that Laclau and Mouffe seek to erect a political theory of discourse. In so doing, they introduce three central concepts – social antagonism, political subjectivity and hegemony – each of which needs to be examined in greater detail.

Antagonisms

Laclau and Mouffe oppose traditional conceptions of social conflict in which antagonisms are understood as the clash of social agents with fully constituted identities and interests. In these approaches, the task of the political analyst is to describe the causes, conditions and resolution of conflict (see Gurr 1970; Duverger 1972; Marx 1977c). Eric Wolf's (1971) classic study of peasant rebellion is a good illustration of this approach. In his comparative account of six 'peasant wars' he argues that the penetration of capitalist relations into 'traditional' peasant communities provided the necessary dislocatory conditions for such events. He then argues that it was the alliances between two groups of social actors – alienated '"rootless" intellectuals', on the one hand, and 'middle peasants and poor, but "free" peasants' on the other – which generated the peasant uprisings themselves.

By contrast, Laclau and Mouffe argue that social antagonisms occur because social agents are *unable* to attain their identities (and therefore their interests), and because they construct an 'enemy' who is deemed responsible for this 'failure'. Hence a reinterpretation of Wolf by Laclau and Mouffe (1985: 125) would suggest that peasants expelled from their land by capitalist farmers and forced to become workers in the city, are literally prevented from 'being peasants' and thus experience a blockage of identity. This 'blockage' or 'failure' of identity is, moreover, a mutual experience for both the antagonizing force and the force that is being antagonized. Thus the task of the discourse analyst is to describe the ways in which the identities of agents are blocked, and to chart the different means by which these obstacles are constructed in antagonistic terms by social agents. In the case of peasants expelled from their land, such an investigation would examine the different ways peasants constructed the landlords or the state as the 'enemy', as well as the different symbolic resources they deployed to oppose such enemies.

Understood in this way, the construction and experience of social antagonisms is central to Laclau and Mouffe's theory of discourse. The mere existence of antagonisms confirms their view that there are no necessary laws of history and no universal political agents motivated by preconstituted interests and identities. Instead, antagonisms introduce social experiences, such as 'failure', 'negativity' or 'lack', which cannot be accounted for by any positive or essentialist logic of society. They also reveal the contingency and precariousness of all identity and social objectivity, as any identity is always threatened by something that is external to it. Their role is thus constitutive of social objectivity, as social formations depend upon the construction of antagonistic relations between social agents 'inside' and 'outside' a social formation (Laclau 1990: 17–18). In this way, antagonisms reveal the boundaries or political frontiers of a social formation, as they show the points where identity can no longer be stabilized in a meaningful system of differences, but is contested by forces which stand at the limit of that order.

Consider the emergence of the Black Consciousness Movement in South Africa during the late 1960s and early 1970s (Howarth 1997). In its formative stages, leaders of this movement constructed a series of antagonistic relationships with different groups within South African society. These included white liberals, the National Party and its apartheid project, as well as other anti-apartheid organizations – the exiled African National Congress and its allies such as the Natal Indian Congress and the Inkatha Movement led by Mangosuthu Buthelezi. Their discourse emphasized that the main 'blockage' to their identity was 'white racism', which systematically denied and prevented the construction and assertion of a black identity. Their political project endeavoured to link together all those who were opposed to apartheid *and* who identified themselves as 'black', rather than 'non-white' or 'non-racial', by instituting a political frontier dividing South African society into two antagonistic camps organized around the black/'anti-black' division (see Biko 1978).

In order to account theoretically for the construction of antagonistic relations, Laclau and Mouffe endeavour to show how a discourse is threatened by an antagonism. They must therefore find a place for a purely negative identity that cannot be represented positively in a given discursive formation, for if it could be represented it would simply be another moment within the existing discourse. Moreover, as this external identity must be a discursive threat, it has to be shared negatively by those interpellated by the discourse. In order to account for this political operation, Laclau and Mouffe introduce the *logic of equivalence*, which consists in the dissolution of the particular identities of subjects within a discourse by the creation of a purely negative identity that is seen to threaten them. Put differently, in the logic of equivalence, if the terms a, b and c are made equivalent ($a \equiv b \equiv c$) with respect to characteristic d, then d must totally negate a, b and c ($d = -(a, b, c)$), thus subverting the original terms of the system. This means that the identity of those interpellated by a discourse would always be split between a set of particular differences conferred by an existing discursive system (a, b, c), and the more universal threat posed by the discursive exterior (d). For example, in the discourse of the Black Consciousness Movement different sections of those oppressed by the apartheid system in South Africa were made equivalent to one another by reference to a common white racism that was seen to negate and block the affirmation of black identity. It was only this shared negation that enabled the movement to build a discursive unity amongst the different ethnic, racial and social groups that had emerged and been fostered under the apartheid system.

By contrast, Laclau and Mouffe (1985: 127–34) introduce the *logic of difference* to account for the expansion of a discursive order by breaking existing chains of equivalence and incorporating the 'disarticulated' elements into the expanding formation. Whereas a project principally employing the logic of equivalence seeks to divide social space by condensing meanings around two antagonistic poles, a project mainly employing a logic of difference attempts to displace and weaken antagonisms, while endeavouring to relegate division to the margins of society (see, for example, Torfing 1998). The discourse of 'Grand Apartheid' or 'separate development' in South Africa can be seen as an extreme example of the logic of difference (Norval 1996). In its heyday, the apartheid project created and imposed a differential system of ethnic and racial particularities on the black population of South Africa. In this extreme example of the logic of difference, the architects of the apartheid system attempted to create a system of differential subject positions, along with a corresponding set of territorial units and political institutions, in an effort to displace demands for a non-racial democratic South Africa. Using a mixture of force and persuasion, they attempted to disrupt the chains of equivalence that national liberation movements such as the African National Congress and Pan-Africanist Congress had constructed between different ethnic groups and social classes opposed to apartheid, and sought to push these movements and their discourses to the margins of society.

Subjectivity and agency

Laclau and Mouffe place great importance on the concepts of subjectivity and agency in developing their conception of discourse.
They emphasize the way in which social actors acquire and live out
their identities, and stress the role of agency in challenging and
transforming social structures. In order to contextualize their
approach let us begin by considering their critique of Althusser's
account of the subject. As I noted in the previous chapter,
Althusser opposes those perspectives that view the subject as an
originator of its own consciousness, or endowed with essential
properties such as economic interests. Instead, he insists that individuals are 'interpellated' or 'recruited' as subjects by ideological
practices. Laclau and Mouffe criticize Althusser's account on two
grounds. First, they contest the view that ideological practices are a
'relatively autonomous' region of a social formation separate from
political and economic practices, arguing that all social practices are
discursive. Second, they oppose his view that subjects are constituted by ideological practices that are in turn determined by underlying social structures, by noting the way in which this reduces the
autonomy of social agents to the mere effects of pre-existing social
structures. In short, while they endorse Althusser's claim that the
identities of subjects are discursively constructed through ideological practices, they do not accept its deterministic and reductionist
connotations.

By contrast, Laclau (1990: 60–1; Laclau and Zac 1984) distinguishes between *subject positions* and *political subjectivity*. As
against a homogenous subject with an essential identity and given
set of interests, the former category refers to the 'positioning' of
subjects within a discursive structure. As there is a plurality of positions with which human beings can identify, an individual actor can
have a number of different subject positions (Laclau and Mouffe
1985: 115). A particular social actor may regard herself as 'black',
'working class', 'Christian' or a 'woman', or a particular combination of these identities, depending on the availability of these
subject positions, a point around which these different subject positions can be articulated and the existence of sustaining practices.

If the concept of subject position accounts for the multiple forms
by which individuals are 'produced' as social actors, the concept of
political subjectivity captures the way in which social actors *act*. In
order to go beyond Althusser's privileging of the structure over the

agent, without recourse, for example, to Giddens's (1984) dualistic conception of structuration theory, Laclau argues that the actions of subjects emerge because of the contingency of the discourses that confer identity on them. This presupposes the category of *dislocation*, which refers to the process by which the contingency of discursive structures comes to be seen (Laclau 1990: 39–41). This 'decentring' of the structure through social processes such as the extension of capitalist relations to new spheres of social life shatters already existing identities and interests, and literally induces an identity crisis for the subject. It is this 'failure' of the structure to confer identity on social actors that 'compels' the subject to act. In this sense, the subject is not simply *determined* by the structure; nor, however, does it *constitute* the structure. The subject is forced to take decisions – or identify with certain political projects and the discourses they articulate – when social identities are in crisis and structures need to be recreated. It is in the process of this *identification* that political subjectivities are created and formed. Once formed and stabilized, they become those subject positions that turn individuals into social actors with certain characteristics and attributes.

Hegemony

Hegemonic practices are important to Laclau and Mouffe's political theory of discourse, as they are an exemplary form of political practice, which involves the linking together of different identities and political forces into a common project, and the creation of new social orders from a variety of dispersed elements. This conception emerges out of a detailed critique of Gramsci's concept of hegemony. In contrast to the Leninist approach, Gramsci's conception of hegemony did not just involve the working class securing a temporary class alliance between distinct class forces and interests, but the transcendence of its narrow corporate interests and the articulation of different social forces in a new historical bloc. In this way, Gramsci (1971: 181–2) envisages the working class transforming its own particular interests into those of 'the people' or 'nation' as a whole, thus becoming a 'collective will' that represents universal values and interests.

Drawing on these insights, Laclau and Mouffe's concept of hegemony has developed in three stages. In their earliest writings, hegemonic practices are conducted by 'fundamental social classes', which aim to transform the state and mode of production in line with their interests and values (Laclau 1977; Mouffe 1979). Here they challenge the Marxist orthodoxy that all ideological elements and interpellations, especially appeals to 'the people' or 'the nation', have a 'necessary class belonging'. Instead, these elements are contingent and can be articulated by competing hegemonic projects, which endeavour to endow them with particular class meanings and connotations.

In the second model, Laclau and Mouffe (1985) argue that the identities of *all* 'ideological' elements and social agents are contingent and negotiable. Indeed, it is only because of the contingency and openness of all social relations that articulatory practices and political agency are possible at all. This is predicated on the distinction between a discursive field of overdetermined identities, on the one hand, and endeavours by different political projects to construct finite and limited discourses on the other. Laclau and Mouffe (1985: 136) specify two further conditions for hegemonic practices to take place. These are the existence of antagonistic forces, and the instability of the political frontiers that divide them. Hegemonic practices thus presuppose a social field criss-crossed by antagonisms, and the presence of contingent elements that can be articulated by opposed political projects striving to hegemonize them.

In this model, then, the major aim of hegemonic projects is to construct and stabilize systems of meaning or 'hegemonic formations' (Laclau and Mouffe 1985: 142). On a societal level, these formations are organized around the articulation of *nodal points*, which underpin and organize social orders. These privileged condensations of meaning confer partially fixed meaning on a particular set of signifiers. For instance, Stuart Hall (1983, 1988) and Andrew Gamble's (1990) analyses of Thatcherism demonstrate the way in which the British Conservative Party transformed itself from a party of consensual 'One Nation Toryism' and a qualified supporter of the welfare state into an advocate of free market economics and radical reformer of the post-war consensus. They show how this new hegemonic project was able to elaborate and institute a new set of nodal points, organized around signifiers such as the 'free economy' and the 'strong state', which was able decisively to reorganize the British state and society, and institute a new discursive configuration.

A third model of hegemony emerges in Laclau's most recent writings (Laclau 1990: 27–31; 1996a; Butler *et al.* 2000). Laclau now extends the contingency of elements to both the subjects of hegemonic projects *and* to social structures, and the latter are understood as 'undecidable' entities, which always presuppose a discursive exterior that both constitutes and threatens its existence. For instance, the system of apartheid can be described as an 'undecidable' structure, not only because it articulated different and competing logics, but also because its identity depended on a series of 'constitutive outsides', which both formed and deformed its various manifestations (Norval 1996: 9–10, 105–9, 124, 139). Laclau (1990: 39–59, 1996a: 43) also emphasizes the concept of *dislocation* to account for the disruption of symbolic orders. Dislocations are events that cannot be symbolized by an existent discursive order, and thus function to disrupt that order. Laclau uses the concept to introduce an 'extra-discursive' dynamism into his conception of society. He concludes that late modern societies are undergoing an 'accelerated tempo' of dislocatory experiences. This increasingly dislocatory condition is explained by reference to processes such as commodification, bureaucratization and globalization, all of which can be seen as the contemporary manifestations of what the Marxist tradition labelled 'combined and uneven development' (Laclau 1989: 72–8).

An important counterpart to the accelerating rhythm of dislocations is a greater role for political subjectivities, which emerge in the 'spaces' opened up by the fracturing of structures, and whose decisions reconstitute dislocated orders. In this regard, Laclau (1990: 60–4) introduces the concepts of myth and social imaginary to capture these new forms of identification. For their part, myths are new 'spaces of representation', which attempt to 'cover over' dislocations. On the other hand, if myths successfully 'cover over' social dislocations and incorporate a wider range of social demands, they are transformed into imaginaries. Laclau (1990: 64) thus defines a collective social imaginary as 'a horizon' or 'absolute limit which structures a field of intelligibility', and he gives examples such as the Christian millennium, the Enlightenment and positivism's conception of progress as examples of these social phenomena.

Philosophical questions

As Laclau and Mouffe's discursive approach to social and political analysis challenges the epistemological and methodological foundations of mainstream social science, it is not surprising that philosophical questions have been at the centre of debate about their work. Critical realists and positivists have claimed that Laclau and Mouffe's approach is idealist, 'textualist' and relativist (Jessop 1982; Geras 1987, 1988, 1990; Woodiwiss 1990; Doyal and Gough 1991). For instance, Anthony Woodiwiss (1990: 108) tries to drive a wedge between Laclau and Mouffe's denial of an extra-discursive realm of objects and their affirmation that all objects are contingent discursive constructs. Arguing that these two commitments corre-spond to the realist/idealist divide respectively, he claims that their approach 'must be idealist'. However, Laclau and Mouffe do not deny the existence of a reality external to thought. What they do contest is the possibility that these real objects have a *meaning* inde-pendently of the discourses in which they are constituted as objects. As Laclau and Mouffe (1985: 108) put it:

> The fact that every object is constituted as an object of discourse has *nothing to do* with whether there is a world external to thought, or with the realism/idealism opposition. An earthquake or the falling of a brick is an event that certainly exists, in the sense that it occurs here and now, independently of my will. But whether their specificity as objects is constructed in terms of 'natural phenomena' or 'expressions of the wrath of God', depends upon the structuring of a discursive field. What is denied is not that such objects exist externally to thought, but the rather different assertion that they could constitute themselves as objects outside any discursive condition of emergence.

In short, while Woodiwiss correctly characterizes Laclau and Mouffe's enterprise as developing a distinctive social ontology, rather than a new methodology or epistemology of the social sci-ences, he offers only idealism and realism as possible ontological options. He thus fails to consider seriously Laclau and Mouffe's proposed 'radical materialism', as a social constructionist alterna-tive to *both* idealism and realism.

At this level of abstraction it should be stressed, moreover, that Laclau and Mouffe's discursive approach is not concerned with the nature of specific types of object, practice, institutions, or even con-crete discourses. In Heidegger's terms, they are not conducting an *ontical* analysis of particular sorts of entities, but are concerned with the necessary presuppositions of *any* inquiry into the nature of objects and social relations (Mulhall 1996: 4). In short, they are con-cerned with *ontological* questions, and seek at this level of inquiry to criticize other ontologies and develop their own alternative. Their aim is thus to affirm the meaningfulness of all objects and practices;

to show that all social meaning is contingent, contextual and relational; and to argue that any system of meaning relies upon a discursive exterior that partially constitutes it. As Laclau (1990) puts it, '[t]he primary and constitutive character of the discursive is . . . the condition of any practice'. For example, their central claim that 'society is an impossible object of analysis' seeks to exclude essentialist, objectivist and topographical conceptions of social relations (whether put forward by positivists, materialists or realists), while developing a relational conception of society in which concepts such as antagonism and dislocation are primary.

Numerous critics have accused discourse theory of relativism. Norman Geras (1990: 99) argues that discourse theory lacks a 'foundation' and thus 'slides into a bottomless, relativist gloom, in which opposed discourses or paradigms are left with no common reference point, uselessly trading blows'. He maintains that 'a pre-discursive reality and an extra-theoretical objectivity form the irreplaceable basis of all rational enquiry, as well as the condition of meaningful communication across and between differing viewpoints'. Thus Laclau and Mouffe's theory jeopardizes the 'most elementary facts of existence', and he asks rhetorically why there are not 'realities of nature, both external and human, which are not merely "given outside" every discourse . . . but the material condition of them all'.

This criticism has to be disaggregated for it contains a cluster of related issues. To begin with, two important aspects have to be separated out. On the one hand, discourse theory analyses the emergence, construction and logic of actual discourses or 'ideologies', and at this level of analysis it is surely indisputable that discourses partially constitute the 'social worlds' of social actors who inhabit society, and that the proponents of these discourses seek to recruit and secure the adherence of social actors to their differing systems of practice (see MacIntyre 1978: 6). Unless one accepts the view that discourses can only be evaluated on epistemological grounds, as is the case with the classical Marxist theory of ideology, then the *de facto* existence of a plurality of discourses renders the need for some ultimate foundation redundant. We are simply confronted with a variety of discourses that are in need of clarification, explanation and evaluation.

On the other hand, discourse theorists are concerned to produce *accounts* of actual discourses. Clearly, the truth claims of these accounts have to be evaluated and it is in this regard that the problem of truth and falsity is pertinent. If the meaning of objects, and the facts about them, depends upon a particular set of background assumptions about the nature of the social world – the postulates of discourse theory – how is it possible to make judgements *within* and *between* competing frameworks? To put it in blunt terms, are all judgements relative to different frameworks, and are all frameworks thus equally valid? (See Rorty 1992b: 166–7.) Underlying Geras's line of questioning are classical epistemological postulates about the relationship between our language and the world, especially the supposition that knowledge depends on some sort of correspondence between statements and facts. It also assumes that all discourses are hermetically sealed, and thus necessarily incommensurable.

Laclau and Mouffe question these presuppositions. First, they do not do away with the truth and falsity of statements *within* paradigms. Rather, in keeping with the philosophies of the later Wittgenstein (1953), Heidegger (1962) and Stanley Cavell (1969), they argue that we have to share some criteria about the meaning of objects and practices *before* we can make knowledge claims about it. Not to share such criteria would be to undermine our ability to refer to different objects and practices in our social worlds. Furthermore, as Foucault (1981) insists, this does not mean that we cannot judge whether some beliefs are true or false in relation to a given 'order of discourse'. It simply means that these judgements depend on the agreed standards of a particular form of life or paradigm in which we find ourselves.

Let us turn to judgements *between* different and perhaps competing forms of life. At the outset, it is important to stress that Laclau and Mouffe do not deny the possibility of comprehending other forms of life, or opposed discourses within the same form of life. However, in order to understand and evaluate other discursive forms we need to understand the logics and reference criteria underpinning them. As discursive forms are intrinsically relational entities, which always refer to other discourses and discursive orders, this is in principle possible and feasible. In other words, it is precisely because discourses can never be hermetically sealed off from one another – their identities are predicated on relationships with other discourses – that there is always the possibility of exchange and communication between them.

Nonetheless, Laclau and Mouffe do. claim that if we are to evaluate different discursive forms it is impossible to command a completely objective point of view. This is because any judgement or evaluation presupposes that one is located within a particular system of meanings and values. It should be stressed that this does not rule out the possibility that some accounts may be *better* than others, or that one can and ought to revise one's position in the light of other perspectives. On the contrary, Laclau and Mouffe's approach purports to offer superior accounts of social and political phenomena by attacking the theoretical assumptions and inconsistencies of competing approaches, and adducing argument and evidence, which would be more *persuasive* than other accounts and interpretations. In conclusion, however, it should be noted that this argument does not overcome the paradoxical consequence that common grounds between paradigms may *not* be constructed. From this point of view, 'incommensurability' between different discursive orders is an inherent possibility that may only be 'resolved' through acts of persuasion or conversion (see Kuhn 1970: 144–59).

Substantive questions

Along with the numerous philosophical challenges to Laclau and Mouffe's approach, there have also been important substantive criticisms. There are at least six, sometimes mutually contradictory, issues that need to be considered in this regard: that Laclau and Mouffe's conception of society reduces social reality to language and 'the text'; that this textual reductionism leads to a complete fragmentation or 'decentring' of social structures; that discourse theory is consequently incapable of analysing social and political institutions; that the approach leads to a complete voluntarism or subjectivism; that the post-structuralist emphases of the approach result in the total reduction of the subject/agent to discursive structures; and that the critique of the concept of ideology by Laclau and Mouffe undermines the critical purchase of discourse theory. These criticisms can be addressed in three groups: the first three concern Laclau and Mouffe's conception of society; the next two objections centre on their conception of subjectivity and agency; and the final objection raises problems of normativity and critique. Let us consider each set in turn.

Laclau and Mouffe's conception of society

The first three objections overlap to the extent that they concern the connection between discursive and non-discursive practices, and touch upon Laclau and Mouffe's conception of society. The criticism that society is 'purely discursive' (Cloud 1994: 227) has already been dealt with in the previous section, where I have shown that the category of discourse does not involve an ontological distinction between 'linguistic' and 'non-linguistic' elements of social life, nor does it entail a sharp distinction between 'ideas' and their 'material' conditions. With respect to their conception of society, it is important to stress at the outset that Laclau and Mouffe's approach depends on the trope of catachresis. That is to say, they 'creatively misapply' the concept of discourse so that it can encompass all dimensions of social reality and not just the usual practices of speaking, writing and communicating. This displacement is, of course, characteristic of a number of different approaches to social and political analysis. One has only to think of the way in which rational choice theorists model social and political behaviour on the behaviour of firms and households in private markets, or the way in which models of communication have been used to develop systems approaches to society and politics.

However, the key issue we have to discuss is how far we can extend Laclau and Mouffe's resultant analogy between language and society. Again, in this regard, it is useful to address this issue at the ontological and ontical levels. It will be recalled, borrowing from Heidegger, that the ontological dimension refers to the implicit assumptions presupposed by any inquiry into specific sorts of phenomena and the ontical level to the specific sorts of phenomena themselves. At the ontological level, Laclau and Mouffe's discursive theory of society and politics is built upon the logics of contingency and necessity, and it is their constant interplay that makes society both possible and impossible. Laclau and Mouffe's analogy between social relations and language at this level yields a number of distinct advantages. To begin with, the structuralist model of language enables them to develop a relational conception of society, which avoids the determinism and reductionism of Marxist and positivist approaches. Moreover, Derrida and Lacan's critique of the structuralist model enables them to show how the 'complex dialectic' between the logics of contingency and necessity can account for the structuring of social relations by hegemonic practices. Finally, the equivalence they make between society and language enables them to draw upon the full range of literary tropes and figures to explain a range of social phenomena and events (Laclau 1998). For instance, they are able to rethink the concepts of social antagonism and 'the structuring of social space' by making use of the logics of equivalence and difference, which are drawn in turn from the difference between paradigmatic and syntagmatic relations in linguistic theory.

On the ontical level, by contrast, their investigation focuses on the characterization of different forms of discourse or kinds of social formation, as well as an explanation of their emergence, functioning and change. It is my contention that existing critiques of Laclau and Mouffe's conception of society fail to make this vital distinction, and consequently fall short of the mark (cf. Howard 1987; Clegg 1989: 178–86; Best and Kellner 1991: 200–4; Aronowitz 1992: 175–92). Nevertheless, there are three areas of Laclau and Mouffe's conception that need further attention. First, they tend to over-emphasize the ontological dimension at the expense of the ontical, which means that their concepts and logics are in danger of appearing too thin and formalistic, and need to be supplemented by a range of thicker concepts and logics. Second, there is some slippage between the two levels of analysis in their writings. For instance, it is not clear from their discussion whether hegemonic practices are applicable to all societies, or whether they are confined to conditions of modernity only (see Laclau and Mouffe 1985: 138). Finally, there is a degree of conceptual imprecision regarding the relationships between certain categories of their ontology, which still need some refinement. Let us consider these claims further.

1. At the outset, the basic constituents of Laclau and Mouffe's social ontology at the ontical level remains too indeterminate. Although they distinguish between 'moments' and 'elements' of a discourse at the ontological level, they do not specify or give examples of these categories. In Laclau's (1977: 92–100) earlier work, 'elements' are explicitly understood as ideological components such as 'militarism', 'statolatry,' 'anti-clericalism', 'nationalism', 'anti-Semitic racism', 'elitism', and so forth, which make up ideological discourses such as Italian Fascism or Peronist populism. However, in his later writings elements are sometimes used in a narrow sense to refer to signifiers such as 'justice', 'order', 'democracy' or 'the free world' (Laclau 1996a: 36–46, 56–65), while at other

times they refer to the central components of any social formation, such as the 'economic', 'political' and 'ideological' dimensions of society (Laclau 1990: 21–6). In the latter formulation, the different dimensions of society are inextricably fused and can only be separated for analytical purposes.

This raises questions about the character of these particular configurations of elements and the grounds for their analytical separation. As a first response, Laclau and Mouffe correctly argue that they do not want to specify the content of these elements at the ontological level, as this would predetermine their character at the ontical level in ways reminiscent of Marxist theory. Nevertheless, this still begs the question about the specification and individuation of elements at the ontical level. That is to say, we need explicit categorizations and descriptions of different sorts of societies, as well as accounts of different types of hegemonic formation either at the 'ideal-typical' or 'empirical' level. In this way, the historical specificity of different types of society can be fully explored. As yet, Laclau and Mouffe have not done this clarifying work.

2. A further difficulty is the way in which Laclau and Mouffe conceive the unity between the different discourses that make up society. In different terminology, this query concerns the production of 'society effects'. This set of criticisms is neatly captured by Žižek's (1989: 154) claim that Laclau and Mouffe's approach emphasizes the constant 'metonymical sliding' of meaning, consonant with post-structuralist philosophies associated with Derrida and Foucault, rather than the production of 'metaphorical cut[s]' characteristic of Lacanian theory. In other terms, Laclau and Mouffe's conception of society privileges 'total contingency, indeterminacy and randomness' and denies 'the necessary limiting effects of extra-discursive material conditions' (Larrain 1994: 104, 101; see also Schatzki 1996: 117–18). This critique is misplaced in the case of Laclau and Mouffe's approach and represents a misreading of post-structuralism in general. Laclau and Mouffe explicitly argue against a complete dissemination and unfixity of meaning, and introduce the category of nodal points to account for the knitting together of different elements into a 'signifying chain'. Signifiers such as the 'free economy' and the 'strong state' in Thatcherist discourse perform the function of organizing the various elements that constituted that discursive formation. Moreover, they insist that the linking together of the various nodal points that form a society *depends* on the drawing of political frontiers

between 'insiders' and 'outsiders'. Hence their approach emphasizes the necessity of 'partial closures' and 'partial fixations' of
meaning in society, which is in keeping with the post-*structuralist*
emphasis on the weakening and deconstruction of structures,
rather than their complete dissolution.

This account is supplemented in Laclau's (1996a) most recent
writings when he introduces the concept of an *empty signifier* to
account for the unity of society. Social formations are now built
around impossible objects of discourse that function to link
together the different elements of social formation in a precarious
unity. For instance, the myth of an embattled nation denied autonomy and self-determination by a hostile power can serve to unify
disparate groups and forces in a society, as is evident in the recent
manifestations of Serbian nationalism. While this model provides
an overarching logic that unifies different nodal points into a
common formation, it does raise a further set of questions. One
possible source of confusion in this model concerns the relationship
between nodal points and empty signifiers. The precise conceptual
relationship between these basic ontological categories has not
been fully articulated and requires greater specification (Norval
2000). Moreover, we are still not clear about the precise ontical
status of 'empty signifiers'. How, for instance, do signifiers such as
'justice', 'blackness' and 'order' function to unify and sediment a
wide range of practices and discourses?

3. A number of commentators emphasize the difficulties of
analysing social and political institutions from a discourse theory
perspective (Jessop 1982; Bocock 1986: 104–17; Bertramsen *et al.*
1990: 65). For example, Nicos Mouzelis (1988: 115, 113) argues that
Laclau and Mouffe's analysis of articulatory practices takes place
'in an institutional vacuum', such that their anti-essentialist account
of discourse means that they are 'unable to deal seriously with
problems related to the constitution, persistence and long-term
transformation of global social formations'. Although writers such
as Mouzelis and Bob Jessop correctly point to the dearth of discursive analyses of institutions and organizations, this critique
needs to be tempered by two factors. First, discourse theorists
strongly reject approaches that account for institutions such as the
state by making reference to transhistorical and objective laws of
historical development, or which treat institutions as unified subjects endowed with interests and capacities. Second, on a more
positive note, discourse theory offers alternative conceptual

resources to analyse and describe institutions and organizations. Institutions are understood as 'sedimented' discourses, which despite their political origins as products of hegemonic practices have become relatively permanent and durable. In this sense, there are no qualitative distinctions between discourses, only differences in their degree of stability.

Consider, for instance, the long-standing debate about the state (or government) in liberal democratic societies. Very schematically, pluralists argue that there are a myriad of competing groups and interests in liberal democratic societies, such that governments are perpetually fragmented and 'open' to different representations, while Marxists presume that there is a dominant social class, which determines both the character and policies of the state in capitalist society (see Jessop 1982; Dunleavy and O'Leary 1987). The exhaustion of this debate in recent times is largely a consequence of the underlying assumptions of the various perspectives. Either society is completely fragmented into competing interests and power is dispersed, or there is a dominant social class, which structures power in its own interests. Laclau and Mouffe's alternative starting point is that there is neither complete determinism nor fragmentation. Instead, the continuous interplay between the logics of necessity and contingency means that the construction of institutions such as the state is the product of competing hegemonic struggles seeking to impose their projects on society.

In this regard, the state may be understood as having different degrees of 'relative autonomy' from different interests and groups in society, thus enabling it to facilitate the reproduction of capitalist relations, while remaining accessible to different, perhaps noncapitalist, representations (see Miliband 1969; Poulantzas 1973). This relative autonomy depends on the balance of political forces in a given historical period, as well as the political projects that manage to institutionalize and sediment the key organizations of society. Conducting research into these precise organizational outcomes and logics, and pinpointing the constraints they exert on social actors and agencies, is precisely the sort of 'ontical research' that discourse theorists must conduct. The investigation of the social and political practices through which degrees of autonomy are constructed, itself premised on the idea that institutions are not determined by something external and objective, opens up an alternative research agenda.

Structure and agency

The second group of criticisms deals with Laclau and Mouffe's conception of subjectivity and political agency. One line of critique suggests that their approach amounts to nothing more than 'an absolute voluntarism' (Rustin 1988: 169) or 'subjectivism', which privileges the role of the human subject above structural constraints (Dallmayr 1989: 131). This line of attack focuses on the way Laclau and Mouffe supposedly give priority to the 'logic of contingency', such that 'almost anything is possible' (Osborne 1991: 210). From a diametrically opposite point of view, doubts have been raised about Laclau and Mouffe's account of political agency. Rastko Močnik (1993: 155) and Slavoj Žižek (1990: 250–1) argue that Laclau and Mouffe's conception of the agent as a Foucauldian 'subject position' within a discursive structure robs the subject of any political agency and substance. Thus the subject is just 'spoken for' by pre-existing discursive structures.

Laclau and Mouffe's perspective on the question of structure and agency has resolutely attempted to find a middle path between these two critical positions. They reject essentialist approaches to subjectivity, in which individuals are deemed simply to maximize their interests, as well as approaches that reduce agency to the role of reproducing preconstituted structures, by insisting that while human beings are constituted as subjects within discursive structures, these structures are inherently contingent and malleable. Moreover, this 'undecidability' is shown in situations of dislocation or disorder when structures no longer function to confer identity. In this situation, when subjects construct and identify with new discourses they become political agents in the stronger sense of the term. In Laclau's (1990: 60–7, 1995) words, political agents emerge when discourses are ruptured and new forms of decision – understood as identifications – are taken.

This reasoning makes a powerful contribution to the structure/agency debate. However, one difficulty concerns the positing of an unconditional subjectivity that is literally able to 'create' meaningful structures. While this conception accounts for extreme or 'limit' situations such as revolutions when a thorough restructuring of social relations may occur, even here Laclau's thesis ought to be qualified by the fact that most revolutionary movements and agents are conditioned by existing ideological traditions and

organizational infrastructures. This qualification is acknowledged
in Laclau's (1990: 65–7) later writings when he argues that certain
discourses need to be 'available' and 'credible' if movements and
political agents are to emerge and construct new social orders.

A second difficulty concerns the question of taking a decision
itself. In this regard, Laclau tends to regard decision-making, the
emergence of political agents and the creation of new social orders
as equivalent. However, this collapses the distinction between
different kinds of decision-making. In this respect, a distinction
needs to be made between decisions taken *within* a structure and
decisions taken *about* a structure, and these two modalities of
decision-making are best viewed as two poles of a spectrum of possible forms of decision-making, in which concrete acts can be located
according to the degrees to which they produce structural effects.
For example, it is evident that consumers in free markets or poli-
ticians in parliaments are continuously taking decisions without
ever questioning or creating new structural contexts in which these
choices are made. However, in revolutionary situations collective
political subjects clearly take decisions about the creation and formation of new social structures. With the kind of qualifications
noted above, these are the situations in which Laclau's novel theorization of structure and agency becomes applicable. What this
means is that, rather than a general theory of a radical political
agency, we need to remain sensitive to the specific historical contexts in which different kinds of subjectivity come into play. The
criterion for this analysis depends on the kinds of decision that
are taken, and the circumstances in which they are taken.

Ideology and the question of critique

Does Laclau and Mouffe's rejection of the traditional Marxist conception of ideology 'undercut the critique of ideology', such that
there can be 'no question of asking where social ideas actually hail
from'? (Eagleton 1991: 219). In other words, does discourse theory
lack a critical edge? (Norris 1993: 289–92) Is there a 'normative
deficit' in Laclau and Mouffe's approach? To begin with, it is
important to note that the concept of ideology does *not* disappear
from Laclau and Mouffe's approach, although (*à la* Foucault) it
does not depend upon the usual epistemological grounding.
Instead, the category of ideology is reserved to describe the desire
for *total* closure by political projects and movements; it consists of

'the non-recognition of the precarious character of any positivity, of the impossibility of any final suture' (Laclau 1983: 24; see also Laclau 1996b). In other words, an 'ideological' discourse fails or refuses to recognize its dependency on a 'constitutive outside', and does not acknowledge its own contingent status. By contrast, Laclau and Mouffe's (1985: 190) own proposal for a plural and radical democracy, built as it is around the extension of demands for liberty and equality into greater and greater areas of social life, seeks to recognize and incorporate a sense of its own contingency and precariousness: 'This moment of tension, of openness, which gives the social its essentially incomplete and precarious nature, is what every project for radical democracy should set out to institutionalize' (see Mouffe 1989, 1992, 1993, 2000).

Critical discussions of Laclau and Mouffe's project for radical democracy have centred on their supposed relativism. If there are no ultimate grounds for defending and justifying any set of values and beliefs, how can they expect to argue for radical democracy? This sort of 'enlightenment blackmail', as Foucault (1984a: 43) puts it, implies that unless one has or invokes absolute foundations to defend a political project, then one has no grounds whatsoever. However, just as most competitors in a game cannot predetermine its outcome yet are still willing to play, so Laclau and Mouffe can argue their case for radical democracy without assuming it to 'trump' any opposition proposal. In other words, it is the actual proposals they (and others) put forward which must be evaluated and not the conditions of possibility for making any judgement at all. On this score, moreover, it is up to opponents of radical democracy to suggest positive and feasible alternatives to radical democracy.

One final question in this regard concerns the alleged 'normative deficit' in Laclau and Mouffe's theory of hegemony (see Žižek 1999: 174). For instance, Simon Critchley (1998: 809) holds that if Laclau and Mouffe's theory of hegemony 'is simply the description of a positively existing state of affairs, then it risks identification and complicity with the logic of contemporary capitalist societies'. He goes on to argue that Laclau and Mouffe's theory runs the risk of 'collapsing into a voluntaristic Schmittian decisionism' and thus needs to be supplemented by an explicitly formulated ethical framework. He draws on the writings of Emmanuel Levinas and Jacques Derrida to develop an ethics of 'infinite responsibility' to the Other (see Critchley 1992).

Critchley is correct to raise questions about the division between describing and evaluating in Laclau and Mouffe's writings. At times, it does appear as if the various logics in their texts are simply analytical tools with little or no normative content, which can be applied to all cases. However, careful inspection of their arguments shows that the theory of hegemony *does* presuppose a certain normative orientation as it emerges out of a critique of Leninism. Whereas Lenin's conception of hegemony is little more than a temporary tactical alliance between classes and groups pursuing a limited end – the overthrow of the Tsarist regime – Laclau and Mouffe invoke the idea of democratic practice and the work of Gramsci to develop a quite distinct political theory. For them, hegemonic practices presuppose a degree of autonomy and difference amongst the different components of an 'alliance', such that the identities of different groups have to be retained. Thus hegemony both requires the modification of identities and interests as a new set of relationships are constructed, as well as the institutionalization of a more universal democratic and pluralist ethic amongst the social actors themselves (Laclau 1992; see also Zerilli 1998, and the discussion in Smith 1998: 177–202). It is equally true that the logic of hegemony has been generalized into a more universal tool of analysis, but its practical and normative implications are clear.

Furthermore, practitioners of discourse theory do not claim to be conducting value-free or 'objective' investigations. It is a basic assumption of the perspective that the discourse theorist is always situated in a particular discursive formation and within a specific tradition, in which he or she has been constituted as a subject just like any other subject. What is challenged is the claim that values can be *derived* or *deduced* from the philosophical assumptions and social ontology of discourse theory. In this sense, a post-foundational perspective does not give rise to a certain set of political and ethical positions, though it does rule some positions out – those based on essentialist presuppositions, for example. The assertion and justification of values are thus the result of an articulatory practice, rather than a necessary entailment.

Conclusion

This chapter has evaluated the post-Marxist approach to discourse theory. I have shown how this approach resolves some of the difficulties pinpointed in classical Marxist accounts of ideology and politics, and I have suggested some future trajectories of theoretical and empirical research in this domain of analysis. One issue that has not been examined, but which looms over any attempt to sketch out a feasible discursive approach to social and political analysis, concerns the methodological requirements of such an enterprise. These requirements include a clarification of the goals of discourse analysis in the social sciences; the concept of theory deployed by discourse analysts; the procedures for conducting research; and the difficulties of applying the abstract logics of discourse theory to empirical cases and the difficulties of making larger inferences from the studies that are carried out. It is to these questions that I now turn.

7

Deploying Discourse Theory

This book has examined the concept of discourse and outlined a particular theory of discourse for social and political analysis. In the first two chapters I presented the genesis of the concept of discourse in the structuralist and post-structuralist traditions of thinking, and in Chapters 3 and 4 evaluated Foucault's distinctive theory of discourse by focusing on the different methodological dimensions of his work. The next two chapters clarified and assessed Laclau and Mouffe's theory of discourse by showing how it resolves some of the difficulties pinpointed in Marxist theories of ideology and politics. This concluding chapter brings together the various threads of my argument by discussing the ways in which discourse theory can be applied to social and political analysis. I begin by locating discourse theory in the wider traditions of inquiry governing research in the social sciences.

Discourse theory, naturalism and hermeneutics

The kind of discursive approach argued for in this book stands squarely against those social scientists who borrow their models of knowledge and methodological procedures from the natural sciences in the belief that the goal of social science is to explain phenomena and events in objective universal terms. In brief, underlying this conception of social science is a particular picture of knowledge as a value-free search for causal accounts of phenomena, which can be empirically tested and confirmed against observation using all available or representative evidence. The overall objective of research in this tradition is the production of universal laws and theories that in Popperian terms are falsifiable, which means they must have the capacity to be confirmed or refuted by independent testing and the production of relevant empirical counterfactuals (Popper 1959). In turn, these universal laws and theories serve as the basis for predicting comparable or future events and processes. As a result of the unquestioned success of the natural sciences in explaining and predicting the physical world, and the promise of a consonant degree of success in the social world, this model of science exerts considerable force on social scientists, and it is evident in intellectual movements such as logical positivism, behaviouralism, and certain forms of structural functionalism, critical realism and Marxism (see Delanty 1997).

In recent decades, however, numerous research programmes have challenged this positivist hegemony by drawing upon a range of interpretative and critical traditions of analysis, such as ethnography, psychoanalysis, deconstruction, post-structuralism, Western Marxism and post-analytical philosophy (Taylor 1971; Dallmayr and McCarthy 1977; Shapiro 1981; Gibbons 1987). For instance, the hermeneutical tradition of inquiry strongly contests positivistic and naturalistic conceptions of social science. Whereas the goal of positivism is the objective explanation of an independently existing reality, hermeneuticists aim to understand and interpret a world of meaningful social practices from the 'inside', that is, rather than viewing 'objective reality' as a 'disengaged spectator', hermeneuticists always find themselves within a world of constructed meanings and practices, and seek to make this world more intelligible. The descriptions and explanations they put forward always presuppose the fact that they are able to understand the objects they are investigating, such that any further explanations and explications are always relative to this ultimate goal.

Arguing from this standpoint, Peter Winch (1990: 22) attacks positivists for attempting to ground their approaches to the social sciences on the methods of natural science. Borrowing partly from Weber's concept of *Verstehen* and the philosophy of the later Wittgenstein, Winch (1990: 22) takes the object of social sciences to be meaningful or 'rule-governed' social behaviour, and stresses the 'central role which the concept of understanding plays in the activities ... characteristic of human societies'. Understanding in this context consists in 'grasping the *point* or *meaning* of what is being said or done', which is 'far removed from the world of statistics and causal laws' and more akin to grasping 'the internal relations that link the parts of a realm of discourse' (Winch 1990: 115).

In keeping with this ethos, philosophers of science such as Thomas Kuhn (1970) have argued that scientific practices, such as conducting experiments, presuppose a set of shared background meanings (or paradigms), which make it possible for natural scientists to determine what counts as an object of inquiry, how results are to be interpreted, which results are to be regarded as true or false, and so on. In the social sciences, according to Winch, the situation is even more complex as both the researchers *and* their objects of research are meaningful practices and social constructions. This means that social scientists have to understand the rules and conventions governing their own practices of inquiry, as well as those governing their objects of inquiry. Hermeneuticists thus argue that social scientists cannot disregard (or 'bracket') the background assumptions which make their research possible, as they are unable to agree conclusively about the appropriate methods with which to proceed (Dreyfus and Rabinow 1993: 35–44). Consequently, unlike the established natural sciences, the social sciences are unable to constitute paradigms in the Kuhnian sense of the term, but are subject to constant disputes not only about their research outcomes, but also about the correct methods with which to proceed in the first place.

For the most part, the kind of discursive approach that I am arguing for in this book concurs with the hermeneutical critique of naturalism. Discourse theory is concerned with understanding and interpreting socially produced meanings, rather than searching for objective causal explanations, and this means that one of the major goals of social inquiry is to delineate the historically specific rules and conventions that structure the production of meanings in particular historical contexts. An approach of this kind thus has affinities with what some anthropological researchers call 'thick description' or culturalist modes of understanding and explanation (see Garfinkel 1967; Geertz 1973; Scott 1985). Such investigations explore how, in what forms, and for what reasons social agents come to identify themselves with particular systems of meaning, as well as the constitution, functioning and transformation of systems of discursive practice.

Nevertheless, despite this significant family resemblance, discourse theory is not synonymous with hermeneutical modes of inquiry. Discourse theory does not simply attempt to retrieve and reconstruct the meanings of social actors, and thus stands opposed to a 'hermeneutics of recovery' in which the principal object of research is to make intelligible meanings that are initially unclear or incomplete (Winch 1964; Taylor 1971). Consequently, it does not follow Charles Taylor's (1971: 32–3) research programme of seeking *just* to reconstitute the common meanings and practices of particular groups and communities, such as radicalized students or 'the counter-culture'. Nor, on the other hand, does it seek to uncover the true underlying meanings of texts and actions, which are deliberately concealed by ideological practices or discourses. What might be called a 'hermeneutics of suspicion', evident in the writings of Marx, Nietzsche or Freud, seeks to uncover some deep truth in practices – whether it be 'class struggle', the 'will to power' or the 'unconscious' – which can 'demystify' surface meanings and appearances (Ricoeur 1970: 35). In this model of analysis, practices and forms of representation are seen merely as distorted expressions of underlying logics and trends, and the task of analysis is clarification, critique and emancipation (Dreyfus and Rabinow 1982: xviii–xix).

Instead, while discourse theory does seek to provide novel interpretations of events and practices by elucidating their meaning, it does so by analysing the way in which political forces and social actors construct meanings within incomplete and undecidable social structures. This is achieved by examining the particular structures within which social agents take decisions and articulate hegemonic projects and discursive formations. Moreover, discourse theorists seek to locate these investigated practices and logics in larger historical and social contexts, so that they may acquire a different significance and provide the basis for a possible critique and transformation of existing practices and social meanings. For example, in Chapter 4 I noted the way in which Foucault provides a new interpretation of the 'repressive hypothesis', which suggests that European history moved from a 'lively frankness' about sexuality in the classical period to a period of growing sexual repression and then finally to a period of 'sexual liberation'. Foucault argues that this narrative both structures the beliefs of those analysing and criticizing systems of power in the name of liberation and is immanent in the practices governing modern society. However, his genealogical critique does not endeavour to uncover the essence of the 'repressive hypothesis' by connecting it to deep mechanisms in our mental apparatus, nor does he accept the self-interpretations articulated by those who hold these beliefs. Instead, by locating this ideological construction within the broader logic of 'bio-power', he shows that it is connected to processes that are not apparent or understood by those who believe in the 'repressive hypothesis'. From this perspective, beliefs about sexual liberation can be seen to be complicit with a more general 'will to power' characteristic of Western societies.

Epistemological issues

This positioning of discourse theory *vis-à-vis* naturalism and hermeneutics still begs a series of questions about the role of theory in producing empirical accounts, as well as the epistemological status of the accounts produced. To begin with, what is the role of theory in interpreting problems, and what is the relationship between theory and its objects of research? Simplifying considerably, social scientists divide theory into two components. Empirical theories aim to provide causal explanations of phenomena by establishing the necessary and sufficient conditions for the occurrence of an event or process, whereas normative theories seek to advocate and justify the key principles around which society is structured. As against this division, discourse theory can be characterized as 'constitutive theory' in that it consists of a framework of consistently related concepts and logics, coupled with a distinctive social ontology which provides a common language to describe, interpret and evaluate social phenomena (Smith 1995: 26–8).

Constitutive theory is thus intimately connected to the social reality it describes and interprets, and cannot be falsified by the accounts of reality it facilitates. Rather, the empirical accounts which discourse theorists produce have to be evaluated as particular interpretations of the research objects they have constructed, and not as confirming or refuting instances of a separately constituted empirical theory (see Culler 1998: 139–40). The ultimate tribunal of this evaluation is the community of scholars who judge the interpretations proffered, and the adequacy or inadequacy of discourse theory as a whole depends on its ability to engender plausible accounts of social phenomena. In this sense, the ultimate criterion for judging the adequacy of the discourse approach as a whole is pragmatic; it can be evaluated by the degree to which it makes possible new and meaningful interpretations of the social and political phenomena it investigates.

Explanation and understanding

In order to substantiate this approach to theory, we need to clarify
the relationship between explanation and understanding, and consider questions about the status of truth and falsity in discourse
theory. If naturalistic accounts of social science place a priority on
the role of explanation, how do discourse theorists conceive the
relationship between explanation and understanding? Following
Winch (1990: x), it is possible to elaborate a more complex relationship between these two aspects by stressing that the process of
explaining social processes requires some form of initial understanding of social phenomena, no matter how partial or fragmen-
tary, otherwise our research objects would not be intelligible, and
the task of explanation is to render these incomplete understandings
more coherent. In this way, explanations couched in the concepts of
a particular theoretical framework, be they 'dislocation', 'antagonism', 'equivalence', 'the other' or 'hegemony', strive to supplement
a less than complete understanding of a given event or process with
a fuller understanding, thus providing a new interpretation.

Does this position result in a vicious circle which only an independent and objective causal account of phenomena can overcome? In keeping with its anti-naturalist stance, discourse theory
opposes causal explanations of social phenomena, which take the
form of subsuming empirical events under universal laws, as in
Hempel's (1966) 'covering law' model, or which depend on the
positing of intrinsic causal properties of objects, as in critical realist
accounts (Bhaskar 1978, 1979). It does not accept that there are universal causal laws in the social sciences comparable with those in
the natural sciences, and it does not conceive the task of the social
scientist as delineating the inherent properties or causal mechanisms of objects. Instead, discourse theorists are concerned with
how, under what conditions, and for what reasons, discourses are
constructed, contested and change. They seek, therefore, to
describe, understand and explain particular historical events and
processes, rather than establish empirical generalizations or test
universal hypotheses, and their concepts and logics are designed for
this purpose.

Consider the interplay between the concepts of dislocation and
antagonism in discourse theory. It will be recalled from Chapter
6 that dislocations are those contingent events that cannot be

symbolized or represented within a discourse, and thus disrupt and destabilize orders of meaning. By contrast, social antagonisms represent particular discursive responses to dislocatory experiences, and whether or not these specific mythical discursive responses become new collective social imaginaries depends on the degree to which they can function as 'spaces of inscription' for a wide variety of heterogeneous demands and identities (Laclau 1990). In other words, dislocatory experiences provide the conditions for the construction of antagonistic relations between agents, but they do not determine the form these discursive constructions take. For instance, it is widely acknowledged that a condition for the emergence of Mrs Thatcher's radical New Right government in the late 1970s and 1980s was the dislocation of the Keynesian welfare state. However, it is equally true that the hegemonic crisis of the post-war consensus in British politics and society did not determine the character of Thatcherite discourse. Determining how and what form Thatcherite discourse took, as well as its consequences for the structuring of social relations, requires careful empirical analysis of the way in which social antagonisms were constructed and political frontiers drawn during the period.

Truth and falsity

Just as discourse theorists stress the ultimate contingency of every social meaning and practice, so their epistemological position rejects essentialist theories of knowledge production. In this respect, as I showed in the previous chapter, their anti-foundational stance is directed against all forms of empiricism, idealism and realism. Generally speaking, as Althusser (Althusser and Balibar 1970: 36–7) puts it, in all these conceptions 'to know is to abstract from the real object its essence, the possession of which by the subject is called knowledge'. In social science terms, this involves obtaining a correct representation of the real world of events and objects. If in idealist versions it is concepts that subsume the empirical content of objects, in empiricist and realist perspectives it is the world of objects and events that ultimately determines the meaning and truth of statements.

By contrast, discourse theorists adopt a more complex stance toward the production of truth and the 'verification' of knowledge. This stance begins from a different conception of the subject and the object, and accepts an irreducible gap between the social world and its perspicuous representation. First, as I noted in Chapter 3, following thinkers in the French epistemological tradition (Canguilhem, Bachelard and Foucault), theoretical objects are never given by the world of experience and facts, but are constructed in historically specific systems of knowledge (see Foucault 1972: 44–5). Second, questions of truth and falsity are not determined by a theory-independent world of objects, but are relative to the standards set down by particular systems of knowledge (Visker 1992). In this respect, discourse theory draws upon a long tradition of thought, stretching back to the writings of Wittgenstein, Heidegger, Kuhn and Foucault, which has questioned the privileging of validity and 'objectivity' over meaning, and made issues of truth relative to systems of meaning (see also Hacking 1983, 1985). Heidegger (1962: 261), for instance, argues that the question of validity, in the usual sense of propositional truth, presupposes a world of meaningful discourse in which we identify and encounter objects in the world. While, therefore, the truth-value of a statement can be decided by its 'correspondence' or 'lack of correspondence' to an 'external reality', this already assumes that there are certain linguistic rules and conventions that define what that external reality is, and how propositions are to be articulated (Foucault 1981: 60–1). This does not imply that there are never disputes about the validity of statements, or that they are in principle unresolvable. It does mean, however, that decisions about the truth and falsity of statements are settled *within* orders of discourse (or paradigms) using criteria established by those orders themselves (see Wittgenstein 1953: propositions 240–1).

Research strategies

In discussing research strategies appropriate to a discourse theory perspective, what in positivist styles of research would be called the process of 'operationalizing' the logics and concepts of discourse theory, it is necessary to stress that there are no purely algorithmic methods and procedures of social science investigation. This does not mean, however, that discourse theory promotes a kind of 'methodological anarchism' or 'irrationalism', as some commentators suggest (see Habermas 1987b; Bhaskar 1989; Geras 1990; Krasner 1996). Rather it implies that, in each instance of concrete research, discourse theorists have to modulate and articulate their concepts to suit the particular problems they are addressing (see

Gasché 1986: 121–4; Laclau 1990: 208–9). Conducting empirical
research is thus akin to 'applying a rule' in the Wittgensteinian
sense of the expression. That is to say, it consists of learning how to
use the same theoretical rules differently to suit the particular historical contexts in which they are to be applied (Wittgenstein 1953:
propositions 198–202; see Tully 1995: 105–11). In this regard, I want
briefly to discuss two styles of applying discourse theory, which are
gleaned from the writings of Foucault and Derrida respectively, and
then examine the way in which research questions can be defined
from within a discourse theory perspective.

Styles of discursive research

Just as Wittgenstein (1953: proposition 133) maintains that there is
no single method of philosophical analysis, so discourse theorists
argue that there is no one method of conducting discourse analysis,
but rather a number of different styles of research compatible with
its social ontology. More specifically, Foucault and Derrida provide
us with two possible styles of applying discourse theory to empirical research topics. As I noted in Chapters 3 and 4, Foucault's various endeavours to clarify his methodological presuppositions led
him to the strategy of problematization. This strategy is 'a matter of
analysing, not behaviour or ideas, nor societies and their "ideologies", but the *problematizations* through which being offers itself to
be, necessarily, thought – and the *practices* on the basis of which
these problematizations are formed' (Foucault 1985: 11). Problematization synthesizes his archaeological and genealogical
dimensions of discourse analysis, in which archaeology makes possible the examination of 'forms themselves' and genealogy enables
him to 'analyse their formation out of the practices and the modifi-
cations undergone by the latter' (Foucault 1985: 11–12).

David Campbell (1998) uses this style of research to examine the
conflict in Bosnia and the disintegration of the former Yugoslavia.
He examines the different ways in which the Bosnian conflict was
problematized by different forces within Bosnia, the former
Yugoslavia and in the international community, and he shows how
the problematization of the Bosnian situation as an intractable
'ethnic' and 'nationalist' conflict became the dominant discursive
articulation. He also demonstrates the catastrophic consequences
of assuming, as many decision-makers and academic commentators
in the international community did, that national communities

need to have 'demarcated territories' and 'fixed identities'. This is because 'inscribing the boundaries that make the installation of the nationalist imaginary possible requires the expulsion from the resultant "domestic" space of all that comes to be regarded as alien, foreign, and dangerous' (Campbell 1998: 13). In this sense, the strategy of problematization carries with it an intrinsically ethical connotation, as it seeks to show that dominant discursive constructions are contingent and political, rather than necessary, and that different ways of conceiving the connections between ethnicity, territoriality and identity need to be actively cultivated.

If an ethos of problematization explores the way in which discursive practices construct and normalize particular representations of issues, Derrida's (1981a: 16) technique of deconstruction is a practice of reading, which takes the written metaphysical text – broadly construed – as its object. As I noted in Chapter 2, his 'double reading' of philosophical texts aims rigorously to reconstruct the dominant logics and intentions of a text, while showing its 'limits' and 'points of closure'. These 'limit-points' enable texts to function as apparently consistent and coherent entities, even though they are themselves intrinsically undecidable and unstable. This deconstructive stance is not a neutral methodological device without substantive and critical implications, as it is informed by the view that metaphysical texts are constituted around the privileging of certain conceptual oppositions and logics, and the repression of others. Derrida's double reading thus aims to pinpoint these oppositions, while endeavouring to reverse and reinscribe their effects by articulating what he calls new conceptual 'infrastructures', which contain and redistribute the oppositions in different ways (Gasché 1986: 142–54).

Anne Marie Smith (1994a, 1994b) carefully uses the Derridean infrastructure of supplementarity to unpick the complex logics by which New Right discourses such as Powellism and Thatcherism operate. She shows how black people in Britain were simultaneously represented as a pure addition (or 'mere supplement'), 'as a wholly foreign population which can simply be "repatriated" back to their "home" countries', as well as a dangerous element that insidiously undermines the 'white British' nation from within (Smith 1994a: 75). By concealing these contradictory logics, New Right discourse functions both to promote white British solidarity in the face of apparent threats, such as decolonization and the spectre of European integration, and maintain the idea of an essential white Britishness

untainted by 'foreignness' and 'otherness'. The task of a deconstructive reading is to expose these dissimulating characteristics of
political discourses and to chart the real material effects they have
on the structuring of social relations.

Defining research questions

I have already noted that for discourse theorists, following in the
tradition of writers such as Foucault and Althusser, objects of
investigation are not given in experience, but constructed within
particular theoretical frameworks. But how are these objects of
investigation defined? What problematizations are 'closed off' and
'opened up' by the theoretical assumptions of this research programme? What are the criteria for selecting empirical case studies?
There are two intersecting areas of investigation that call for special
attention within discourse theory. They are the formation and dissolution of political identities, and the analysis of hegemonic practices which endeavour to produce social myths and collective
imaginaries. Both these objects of investigation are premised on the
centrality of social antagonisms in constituting identity and social
objectivity by the drawing of political frontiers between social
agents (see Laclau 1994; Howarth *et al.* 2000).

In order to consider the way in which research objects are defined
and addressed, I will concentrate on Aletta Norval's (1990, 1994,
1996) recent accounts of apartheid discourse. In *Deconstructing
Apartheid Discourse*, she opposes accounts that reduce the
apartheid system to the irrational racial prejudices of embattled
Afrikaner nationalists, or to the economic interests of an emergent
Afrikaner petty bourgeoisie. She also rejects those studies which
have conceded a determining role to underlying logics of capitalist
development, or which have attempted an uneasy synthesis of
racial and class variables (see Wolpe 1988). Instead, Norval (1996:
2) proposes to treat her object of analysis as a politically constructed and complex discursive formation:

> Rather than trying to penetrate below the surface of apartheid, this
> study takes as its object of investigation the discourse of apartheid: the
> multifarious practices and rituals, verbal and non-verbal, through
> which a certain sense of reality and understanding of society were con-
> stituted and maintained.

Viewing apartheid as a discourse means that she does not reduce its specificity to a spurious 'objectivity', and enables her to analyse its changing 'horizon of meanings, conventions and practices, and the . . . modes of subjectivization instituted by it' (Norval 1996: 7).

Framed in these terms, Norval's research questions focus on how and under what conditions the apartheid project – and not other projects with different modes of social division – was able to hegemonize the field of discursivity in South Africa. She endeavours to answer these questions by analysing the various elements that constituted apartheid discourse with a view to discovering its underlying grammar and *modus operandi*. This includes a historical survey of the National Party's propaganda, an analysis of speeches and statements made by the 'organic intellectuals' of the nascent Afrikaner nationalist movement, and a consideration of key official documents, such as the various Commissions of Inquiry, which provided the intellectual framework for the emergence of the apartheid programme. This entails the laborious task of gathering information from largely unused archival sources in order to construct an inventory of the key statements of the apartheid project. Although the form of the data is largely textual, Norval is intent to show how these texts functioned to create, interpellate and mobilize subjects, and her account stresses the practical effects of this discourse on the construction of social meanings, identities and social divisions in the South African context.

In so doing, Norval traces the interacting logics of equivalence and difference by which the political frontiers of apartheid were drawn and redrawn. As against segregationist discourses of the 1920s and 1930s, which were based on a clear black/white frontier, apartheid complicated this basic division by overlaying it with a discourse of ethnic and national difference. She shows how in the 1940s apartheid discourse was the means for establishing a distinctive and particularistic Afrikaner identity. Thus, the unity of the fragmented Afrikaner *volk* (people) was forged by reference to a series of 'others' (the *swart gevaar* or 'black peril', British imperialists, English-speaking capitalists) who were represented as denying and preventing the creation of an Afrikaner identity. During the 1960s and 1970s, Norval shows how this mythical discursive logic was extended to all ethnic and national groups in South Africa, such that all *volkere* (peoples) were 'accommodated' as differential positions in the apartheid system. This period of 'Grand Apartheid' witnessed the predominance of a logic of difference, as the various ethnic and national groups were allocated separate identities, and concomitant political forms of identification. It was not until the rebirth of political resistance to the apartheid system in the 1970s and 1980s, especially after the dislocation of the Soweto uprisings, that new political frontiers were instituted around different divisions, namely, between 'white' and 'black' and between 'apartheid' and 'the people' (see Howarth 2000).

The value of Norval's study is that she provides a new interpretation of apartheid discourse, which contests existing theoretical and empirical accounts. She locates a crucial 'undecidability' in the political frontiers by which apartheid was constructed and functioned, namely the logics of simultaneously excluding and including that which was 'other' in the discourse, and offers new descriptions of its practices, policies and ideas. Her arguments also challenge the underlying 'paradigms' – evident in the so-called 'race/class debate' – that have structured academic and political discussions about South African politics. However, as Norval's study concentrates exclusively on apartheid discourse, social scientists may raise questions about the possibility of making larger inferences and generalizations from a single case study. In brief, does her account of South African politics – and by extension other discursive accounts of single cases – restrict itself to providing descriptions and analyses of that case alone? Does this constraint weaken its overall explanatory power and preclude the analysis of comparative phenomena?

These are important and legitimate queries that discourse analysts ought to be able to answer. Norval's response is to stress the *exemplary* status of the South African case for an exploration of racial and ethnic divisions and identifications, which has clear affinities to what Harry Eckstein (1975: 127) calls 'crucial case studies' that can at times 'score a clean knockout over a theory'. Indeed, many discourse theorists select exemplary or crucial cases precisely so that they can explore more general logics of identity formation and hegemonic practice (see Campbell 1998: ix–xi). Moreover, the logics and descriptions that are 'discovered' in each particular case can be 'tested' in different contexts. This leads, of course, to questions about comparative method (see Landman 2000). Can discourse theorists make use of the comparative method? While I believe the answer is a clear 'yes', there are two caveats that need to be added in this regard. To begin with, the cases to be compared must initially be described, analysed and interpreted on their own terms, as singular instances with their own unique specificity. Second, the point of comparison is to further our understanding and explanation of different logics of identity formation and hegemonic practice in different historical conjunctures, and not to construct generally applicable laws of social and political behaviour.

Conclusion: The heuristics of discursive investigation

In order to draw together these various reflections on the methods and styles of discourse analysis, I shall conclude by summarizing and formalizing the various steps of conducting empirical research from a discourse-theoretical perspective. This is not meant to be a programmatic statement of *the* discursive method of analysis. Such a desire is incompatible with the philosophical assumptions of this perspective. Instead, it is best viewed as a series of heuristic devices to get research under way. Moreover, it should be stressed that discourse theorists seek to circumvent the difficulties they perceive in theoreticist, positivist and empiricist forms of social science research. Put briefly, while they acknowledge the central role of theoretical frameworks in forming their objects of research, they seek to avoid the subsumption of empirical cases under abstract concepts and logics, that is to say, instead of applying theory mechanically to empirical objects, or testing theories against empirical reality, discourse theorists argue for the *articulation* and *modification* of concepts and logics in each particular research context. The condition for this conception of conducting research is that the theoretical framework must be sufficiently 'open' and flexible enough to be 'stretched' and restructured in the process of application. This conception thus excludes essentialist and reductionist theories of society, which tend to predetermine the outcomes of research.

The overall *aim* of social and political analysis from a discursive perspective is to describe, understand, interpret and evaluate carefully constructed objects of investigation. Although the task of understanding and interpreting meaningful practices is the overall objective of discourse analysis, this does not rule out the necessity for explanation. Explanations are necessary to account for incomplete or misleading understandings and to redescribe phenomena in new terms. Nevertheless, explanations are strictly internal to the goal of understanding, interpretation and evaluation, and are couched in the concepts and logics of discourse theory. Moreover, while discourse analysts tend to focus on exemplary or crucial case studies, this does not mean that they cannot make larger claims and inferences, which can be explored and 'tested' in further research. Nor do discourse analysts rule out comparative forms of research. The comparative analysis of cases is a fruitful methodological device, as long as it is made commensurate with the overall onto-logical and theoretical assumptions of discourse analysis.

The critical process of *problematizing* social and political phenomena arises from the social and political practices within which the researcher is located, the inadequacies of existing interpretations of social phenomena, and the intuitions and hunches that the researcher has about the phenomena under con-sideration. The task of problematization is to transform these hunches and intuitions into practical and manageable research questions. This consists in the production of hypotheses; the examination of existing interpretations and the deconstruction of their problematic assumptions and concepts; and the construction of an alternative theoretical framework with which to analyse a research question, drawing upon the concepts and logics of dis-course theory.

The various *qualitative methods* used by discourse analysts to generate and collect empirical material share an important set of family resemblances with historical, ethnographic and anthropo-logical forms of research. Discourse analysts thus gather primary information from a range of possible sources, which include surveys of newspapers, official reports, 'unofficial' documents such as pam-phlets, organizational minutes and agendas, personal biographies and media representations such as television documentaries and films. They also supplement these more narrowly textual modes of investigation by making use of in-depth interviews and ethno-graphic forms of investigation such as participation-observation, and by investigating the structural features of the contexts that limit, but do not determine, social and political possibilities. In all these respects, discourse analysts have to be sensitive to the theor-etical postulates governing their research practices. For instance, discourse analysts using in-depth interviewing have to be aware of the ways in which social subjects retrospectively construct narra-tives in particular ways, the role of the interviewer's own subjec-tivity in staging and organizing the interview, and the changing power relations between interviewer and interviewee.

The *analysis* of empirical data involves three basic operations. These are, firstly, the 'translation' of information into textual form. This means that discourse analysts treat a wide range of linguistic and non-linguistic data as 'texts' or 'writing', thus enabling them to deploy a number of techniques and methods in linguistic and literary theory commensurate with the ontological assumptions of discourse theory. The second operation consists in the application of constructed theoretical frameworks to the problematized object of investigation. As I have already noted, this involves the articulation and modification of abstract concepts and logics to a particular case. In this regard, these concepts and logics demand systematic historical specification as they are deployed. The last element involved in analysing empirical materials concerns the deployment of the various techniques of discourse analysis to the problem investigated.

The *strategy of presenting* the empirical results of research is an important though under-emphasized concern amongst discourse analysts. Disputes about the presentation and justification of results, on the one hand, and the logic and context of their discovery, on the other, abound in the social and natural sciences (Chalmers 1982: 35). Suffice it to say that from a discursive point of view the mode of presentation is integrally connected to the justification of arguments made in its name. Thus a typical discursive study would begin with a critique of existing theoretical and empirical positions, from which it would develop an alternative framework of analysis with which to problematize and address a given object of analysis. This elaboration would involve a deconstruction of the problematic assumptions structuring existing approaches and the articulation of appropriate concepts and logics from the discursive approach. The study would then present the substantive empirical conclusions and arguments produced by the application of the theoretical framework to the problem explored. In so doing, it would have to demonstrate the leverage that such an approach and its substantive conclusions bring to its specific topic of research.

The *confirmation or refutation* of the substantive conclusions reached by discourse analysts depends ultimately on their persuasiveness to the community of researchers and scholars in the social sciences. These judgements will, of course, depend on the degree to which discursive accounts meet the requirements of consistency and coherence in conducting their studies, as well as the extent to which they add new and interesting insights to their various objects of investigation.

The community of critical discourse analysts and the wider community of social scientists form the *ultimate tribunal of truth* for social science investigation. They also act as the stimulants for further research. These judgements are likely, in turn, to point out the need for further investigation or more theoretical refinement. Such a demand for what positivist researchers call a process of 'retroduction' will usually require a new set of relays between the theoretical framework and the empirical materials examined. At this stage, further research may lead to a refinement and modification of the proposed conclusions, the need for comparative research of similar or different cases, the construction of typologies of phenomena and the proposal of middle-range empirical generalizations in need of empirical confirmation or refutation. In sum, the overall objective of discourse-theoretical empirical research is the production of novel and plausible interpretations of selected cases and problems. These accounts need to add new insights into the understanding of a given range of social and political phenomena, to provide the grounds for further empirical research into different but related issues, and to open up new spaces for critical evaluation and political engagement.

References

Adorno, T. and Horkheimer, M. (1973) *Dialectic of Enlightenment*. London: Allen Lane.

Althusser, L. (1969) *For Marx*. London: Allen Lane.

Althusser, L. (1971) *Lenin and Philosophy and Other Essays*. London: New Left Books.

Althusser, L. and Balibar, É. (1970) *Reading Capital*. London: New Left Books.

Anderson, P. (1983) *In the Tracks of Historical Materialism*. London: Verso.

Apter, D. (1987) *Rethinking Development: Modernization, Dependency, and Postmodern Politics*. London: Sage.

Apter, D. (ed.) (1997) *The Legitimization of Violence*. London: Macmillan.

Aronowitz, S. (1992) *The Politics of Identity: Class, Culture and Social Movements*. London: Routledge.

Austin, J. L. (1975) *How to Do Things with Words*. Oxford: Oxford University Press.

Bachelard, G. (1984) *The New Scientific Spirit*. Boston: Beacon Press.

Balibar, É. (1970) 'On the basic concepts of historical materialism', in L. Althusser and É. Balibar, *Reading Capital*. London: New Left Books.

Barrett, M. (1991) *The Politics of Truth*. Cambridge: Polity.

Barthes, R. (1973) *Mythologies*. London: Paladin Books.

Bennington, G. (1993) *Jacques Derrida*. Chicago: Chicago University Press.

Benton, T. (1984) *The Rise and Fall of Structural Marxism: Althusser and His Influence*. London: Macmillan.

Benveniste, E. (1971) *Problems in General Linguistics*. Miami, FL: University of Miami Press.

Bertramsen, R. B., Thomsen, J. P. F. and Torfing, J. (1990) *State, Economy and Society*. London: Unwin Hyman.

Best, S. and Kellner, D. (1991) *Postmodern Theory: Critical Interrogations*. London: Macmillan.

Bhaskar, R. (1978) *A Realist Theory of Science*. Brighton: Harvester.

Bhaskar, R. (1979) *The Possibility of Naturalism: A Philosophical Critique of the Contemporary Human Sciences*. Brighton: Harvester.

Bhaskar, R. (1989) *Reclaiming Reality*. London: Verso.

Biko, S. (1978) *I Write What I Like*. Harmondsworth: Penguin.

Bobbio, N. (1988) 'Gramsci and the concept of civil society' in J. Keane (ed.) *Civil Society and the State: New European Perspectives*. London: Verso.

Bocock, R. (1986) *Hegemony*. London: Tavistock.

Brown, B. and Cousins, M. (1980) 'The linguistic fault: the case of Foucault's archaeology', *Economy and Society*, 9(3): 251–78.

Burman, E. and Parker, I. (eds) (1993) *Discourse Analytic Research*. London: Routledge.

Butler, J., Laclau, E. and Žižek, S. (2000) *Contingency, Hegemony and Universality: Contemporary Dialogues on the Left*. London: Verso.

Callinicos, A. (1989) *Against Postmodernism: A Marxist Critique*. Cambridge: Polity Press.

Campbell, D. (1992) *Writing Security: United States Foreign Policy and the Politics of Identity*. Manchester: Manchester University Press.

Campbell, D. (1998) *National Deconstruction: Violence, Identity, and Justice in Bosnia*. Minneapolis: University of Minnesota Press.

Canguilhem, G. (1989) *On the Normal and the Pathological*. New York: Zone.

Castells, M. (1977) *The Urban Question: A Marxist Approach*. London: Edward Arnold.

Cavell, S. (1969) *Must We Mean What We Say? A Book of Essays*. Cambridge: Cambridge University Press.

Chalmers, A. (1982) *What Is This Thing Called Science? An Assessment of the Nature and Status of Science and its Methods*, 2nd edn. Milton Keynes: Open University Press.

Clegg, S. R. (1989) *Frameworks of Power*. London: Sage.

Clifford, J. (1980) 'On orientalism', *Theory and History*, 19: 204–23.

Clifford, J. (1988) *The Predicament of Culture: Twentieth-Century Ethnography, Literature, and Art*. Cambridge, MA: Harvard University Press.

Cloud, D. L. (1994) '"Socialism of the mind": the new age of post-Marxism' in H. W. Simons and M. Billig (eds) *After Postmodernism: Reconstructing Ideology Critique*. London: Sage.

Connolly, W. E. (1991) *Identity/Difference: Democratic Negotiations of Political Paradox*. Ithaca, NY: Cornell University Press.

Connolly, W. E. (1993) *The Terms of Political Discourse*, 3rd edn. Oxford: Basil Blackwell.

Coulthard, M. (1977) *An Introduction to Discourse Analysis*. London: Longman.

Coward, R. and Ellis, J. (1977) *Language and Materialism: Developments in Semiology and the Theory of the Subject*. London: Routledge & Kegan Paul.

Critchley, S. (1992) *The Ethics of Deconstruction: Derrida and Levinas*. Oxford: Blackwell.

Critchley, S. (1998) 'Metaphysics in the dark: a response to Richard Rorty and Ernesto Laclau', *Political Theory*, 26(6): 803–17.

Culler, J. (1974) 'Introduction' in F. de Saussure, *Course in General Linguistics*. London: Fontana.

Culler, J. (1976) *Saussure*. London: Fontana.

Culler, J. (1983) *On Deconstruction: Theory and Criticism after Structuralism*. London: Routledge & Kegan Paul.

Culler, J. (1998) *Framing the Sign: Criticism and its Institutions*. Oxford: Basil Blackwell.

Cutler, A., Hindess, B., Hirst, P. Q. and Hussain, A. (1977) *Marx's Capital and Capitalism Today*. London: Routledge & Kegan Paul.

Dallmayr, F. (1989) *Margins of Political Discourse*. Albany: State University of New York Press.

Dallmayr, F. and McCarthy, T. (1977) *Understanding and Social Inquiry*. Notre Dame, IN: University of Notre Dame Press.

Dant, T. (1991) *Knowledge, Ideology and Discourse: A Sociological Perspective*. London: Routledge.

De George, R. and De George, F. (1972) *The Structuralists: From Marx to Lévi-Strauss*. New York: Doubleday.

Delanty, G. (1997) *Social Science: Beyond Constructivism and Realism*. Buckingham: Open University Press.

Derrida, J. (1973) *Speech and Phenomena, and Other Essays on Husserl's Theory of the Sign*. Evanston, IL: Northwestern University Press.

Derrida, J. (1976) *Of Grammatology*. Baltimore, MD: Johns Hopkins University Press.

Derrida, J. (1978a) *Writing and Difference*. London: Routledge.

Derrida (1978b) *Edmund Husserl's Origin of Geometry: An Introduction*. Lincoln: University of Nebraska Press.

Derrida, J. (1981a) *Positions*. Chicago: University of Chicago Press.

Derrida, J. (1981b) *Dissemination*. Chicago: University of Chicago Press.

Derrida, J. (1982) *Margins of Philosophy*. Brighton: Harvester Press.

Derrida, J. (1986) 'But, beyond . . . (Open letter to Anne McClintock and Rob Nixon)', *Critical Inquiry*, 13: 155–70.

Derrida, J. (1988a) *Limited Inc*, Evanston, IL: Northwestern University Press.

Derrida, J. (1988b) 'Letter to a Japanese friend' in D. Wood and R. Bernasconi (eds) *Derrida and Difference*. Evanston, IL: Northwestern University Press.

Derrida, J. (1992) *The Other Heading: Reflections on Today's Europe*. Bloomington: Indiana University Press.

Derrida, J. (1994) *Spectres of Marx: The State of Debt, the Work of Mourning, and the New International*. London: Routledge.

Derrida, J. (1997) ' "To do justice to Freud": The history of madness in the age of psychoanalysis' in A. I. Davidson (ed.) *Foucault and his Interlocutors*. Chicago: University of Chicago.

Dews, P. (1987) *Logics of Disintegration: Essays on Contemporary European Philosophy*. London: Verso.

Doyal, A. and Gough, I. (1991) *A Theory of Human Need*. London: Macmillan.

Dreyfus, H. and Rabinow, P. (1982) *Michel Foucault: Beyond Structuralism and Hermeneutic*. Brighton: Harvester.

Dreyfus, H. and Rabinow, P. (1993) 'Can there be a science of existential structure and social meaning?' in C. Calhoun, E. LiPuma and M. Postone (eds) *Bourdieu: Critical Perspectives*. Cambridge: Polity Press.

Dryzek, J. (1994) *Discursive Democracy: Politics, Policy and Political Science*. Cambridge: Cambridge University Press.

Dryzek, J. (1997) *The Politics of the Earth: Environmental Discourses*. Oxford: Oxford University Press.

Dunleavy, P. and O'Leary, B. (1987) *Theories of the State: The Politics of Liberal Democracy*. London: Macmillan.

Duverger, M. (1972) *The Study of Politics*. London: Nelson.

Dyrberg, T. B. (1997) *The Circular Structure of Power*. London: Verso.

Eagleton, T. (1991) *Ideology: An Introduction*. London: Verso.

Eckstein, H. (1975) 'Case-study and theory in political science' in F. I. Greenstein and N. W. Polsby (eds) *Handbook of Political Science*, Volume 1: *Political Science: Scope and Theory*. Reading: Addison-Wesley.

Fairclough, N. (1989) *Language and Power*. London: Longman.

Fairclough, N. (1992) *Discourse and Social Change*. Cambridge: Polity.

Fairclough, N. (2000) *New Labour, New Language?* London: Routledge.

Fairclough, N. and Wodak, R. (1997) 'Critical discourse analysis' in T. van Dijk, *Discourse as Social Interaction*. London: Sage.

Femia, J. (1981) *Gramsci's Political Thought: Hegemony, Consciousness and the Revolutionary Process*. Oxford: Clarendon Press.

Feyerabend, P. (1975) *Against Method*. London: Verso.

Finlayson, A. (1999) 'Language' in F. Ashe, A. Finlayson, M. Lloyd, *et al.* (eds) *Contemporary Social and Political Theory*. Buckingham: Open University Press.

Foucault, M. (1970) *The Order of Things: An Archaeology of the Human Sciences*. London: Tavistock.

Foucault, M. (1972) *The Archaeology of Knowledge*. London: Tavistock.

Foucault, M. (1973) *The Birth of the Clinic: An Archaeology of Medical Perception*. London: Tavistock.

Foucault, M. (1977) *Discipline and Punish: The Birth of the Prison*. New York: Pantheon.

Foucault, M. (1978) 'Politics and the study of discourse', *Ideology and Consciousness*, 3: 7–26.

Foucault, M. (1979a) *The History of Sexuality, Vol. 1: Introduction*. Harmondsworth: Penguin.

Foucault, M. (1979b) 'My body, this paper, this fire', *Oxford Literary Review*, 4(1): 9–28.

Foucault, M. (1980a) *Power/Knowledge: Selected Interviews and Other Writings 1972–1977*. New York: Pantheon.

Foucault, M. (1980b) 'The history of sexuality: an interview with Michel Foucault', *Oxford Literary Review*, 4(2): 3–14.

Foucault, M. (1981) 'The order of discourse' in R. Young (ed.) *Untying the Text: A Post-structuralist Reader*. London: Routledge & Kegan Paul.

Foucault, M. (1982) 'The subject and power' in H. Dreyfus and P. Rabinow, *Michel Foucault: Beyond Structuralism and Hermeneutics*. Brighton: Harvester.

Foucault, M. (1984a) 'What is Enlightenment?' in P. Rabinow (ed.), *The Foucault Reader*. Harmondsworth: Penguin.

Foucault, M. (1984b) 'Polemics, politics and problemizations: an interview', in P. Rabinow (ed.) *The Foucault Reader*. Harmondsworth: Penguin.

Foucault, M. (1985) *The History of Sexuality, Vol. 2: The Use of Pleasure*. New York: Pantheon.

Foucault, M. (1987) 'Nietzsche, genealogy, history' in P. Rabinow (ed.) *The Foucault Reader*. Harmondsworth: Penguin.

Foucault, M. (1988) 'Politics and reason' in L. D. Kritzman (ed.) *Michel Foucault. Politics, Philosophy, Culture: Interviews and Other Writings, 1977–1984*. London: Routledge.

Foucault, M. (1990) *The History of Sexuality, Vol. 3: The Care of the Self*. Harmondsworth: Penguin.

Foucault, M. (1991a) 'Politics and the study of discourse' in G. Burchell, C. Gordon and P. H. Miller (eds) *The Foucault Effect: Studies in Governmentality*. Hemel Hempstead: Harvester Wheatsheaf.

Foucault, M. (1991b) 'The ethic of care for the self as a practice of freedom' in J. Bernauer and D. Rasmussen (eds) *The Final Foucault*. Cambridge, MA: MIT Press.

Foucault, M. (1998) 'On the archaeology of the sciences: response to the epistemology circle' in J. D. Faubion (ed.) *Michel Foucault: Aesthetics, Method and Epistemology*. New York: New Press.

Fowler, R. (1981) *Literature as Social Discourse: The Practice of Linguistic Criticism*. London: Batsford Academic.

Frank, M. (1989) *What is Neostructuralism?*. Minneapolis: University of Minnesota Press.

Frank, M. (1992) 'On Foucault's concept of discourse' in T. J. Armstrong (ed.) *Michel Foucault: Philosopher*. Hemel Hempstead: Harvester Wheatsheaf.

Gamble, A. (1990) *The Free Economy and the Strong State*. London: Macmillan.

Garfinkel, H. (1967) *Studies in Ethnomethodology*. Englewood Cliffs: Prentice Hall.

Gasché, R. (1986) *The Tain of the Mirror: Derrida and the Philosophy of Reflection*. Cambridge, MA: Harvard University Press.

Geertz, C. (1973) *The Interpretation of Cultures*. New York: Basic.

George, J. (1994) *Discourses of Global Politics*. Boulder, CO: Lynne Riener.

Geras, N. (1987) 'Post-Marxism?', *New Left Review*, 163: 40–82.

Geras, N. (1988) 'Ex-Marxism without substance: a rejoinder', *New Left Review*, 169: 34–61.

Geras, N. (1990) *Discourses of Extremity: Radical Ethics and Post-Marxist Extravagances*. London: Verso.

Gibbons, M. (1987) 'Interpreting politics' in M. Gibbons, *Interpreting Politics*. New York: New York University Press.

Giddens, A. (1984) *The Constitution of Society: Outline of a Theory of Structuration*. Cambridge: Polity Press.

Gramsci, A. (1971) *Prison Notebooks*. London: Lawrence and Wishart.

Gurr, T. R. (1970) *Why Men Rebel*. Princeton, NJ: Princeton University Press.

Gutting, G. (1989) *Michel Foucault's Archaeology of Scientific Reason*. Cambridge: Cambridge University Press.

Habermas, J. (1978) *Knowledge and Human Interests*. London: Heinemann Educational.

Habermas, J. (1984) *The Theory of Communicative Action, Vol. 1. Reason and the Rationalization of Society*. London: Heinemann.

Habermas, J. (1987a) *The Theory of Communicative Action, Vol. 2: Lifeworld and System: A Critique of Functionalist Reason*. Cambridge: Polity Press.

Habermas, J. (1987b) *The Philosophical Discourse of Modernity: Twelve Lectures*. Cambridge: Polity.

Hacking, I. (1983) *Representing and Intervening: Introductory Topics in the Philosophy of Natural Science*. Cambridge: Cambridge University Press.

Hacking, I. (1985) 'Styles of scientific reasoning' in J. Rajchman and C. West (eds) *Post-analytical Philosophy*. New York: Columbia University Press.

Hajer, M. (1995) *The Politics of Environmental Discourse: Ecological Modernization and the Policy Process*. Oxford: Clarendon Press.

Hall, P. (1998) *Cultures of Inquiry: From Epistemology to Discourse in Sociohistorical Research*. Berkeley: University of California Press.

Hall, S. (1983) 'The great moving right show' in S. Hall and M. Jacques (eds) *The Politics of Thatcherism*. London: Lawrence and Wishart.

Hall, S. (1988) *The Hard Road to Renewal*. London: Verso.

Hall, S. (1996) 'The problem of ideology: Marxism without guarantees' in D. Morley and K.-H. Chen, *Stuart Hall: Critical Dialogues in Cultural Studies*. London: Routledge.

Hall, S. (ed.) (1997) *Representation*. London: Sage.

Harré, R. (1979) *Social Being: A Theory for Social Psychology*. Oxford: Basil Blackwell.

Harré, R. and Madden, E. H. (1975) *Causal Powers: A Theory of Natural Necessity*. Oxford: Basil Blackwell.

Harris, R. (1988) *Language, Saussure and Wittgenstein: How to Play Games with Words*. London: Routledge.

Harvey, N. and Halverson, C. (2000) 'The secret and the promise: women's struggles in Chiapas' in D. Howarth, A. J. Norval and Y. Stavrakakis (eds) *Discourse Theory and Political Analysis: Identities, Hegemonies and Social Change*. Manchester: Manchester University Press.

Hawkes, T. (1977) *Structuralism and Semiotics*. London: Routledge & Kegan Paul.

Heidegger, M. (1962) *Being and Time*. Oxford: Basil Blackwell.

Heidegger, M. (1985) *History of the Concept of Time*. Bloomington: Indiana University Press.

Hempel, C. G. (1966) *Philosophy of Natural Science*. Englewood Cliffs: Prentice Hall.

Hirst, P. (1979) *On Law and Ideology*. London: Macmillan.

Hjelmslev, L. (1963) *Prolegomena to a Theory of Language*. Madison: University of Wisconsin Press.

Holdcroft, D. (1991) *Saussure: Signs, System, and Arbitrariness*. Cambridge: Cambridge University Press.

Howard, D. (1987) 'The possibilities of a post-Marxist radicalism', *Thesis Eleven*, 16: 69–84.

Howarth, D. (1997) 'Complexities of identity/difference: the ideology of black consciousness in South Africa', *Journal of Political Ideologies*, 2(1): 51–78.

Howarth, D. (1998) 'Discourse theory and political analysis' in E. Scarborough and E. Tanenbaum (eds) *Research Strategies in the Social Sciences: A Guide to New Approaches*. Oxford: Oxford University Press.

Howarth, D. (1999) 'Paradigms gained? A critique of theories and explanations of democratic transition in South Africa' in D. Howarth and A. J. Norval (eds) *South Africa in Transition: New Theoretical Perspectives*. London: Macmillan.

Howarth, D. (2000) 'The difficult emergence of a democratic imaginary: black consciousness and non-racial democracy in South Africa' in D. Howarth, A. J. Norval and Y. Stavrakakis (eds) *Discourse Theory and Political Analysis: Identities, Hegemonies and Social Change*. Manchester: Manchester University Press.

Howarth, D., Norval, A. J. and Stavrakakis, Y. (eds) (2000) *Discourse Theory and Political Analysis: Identities, Hegemonies and Social Change*. Manchester: Manchester University Press.

Jakobson, R. (1990) *On Language*. Cambridge, MA: Harvard University Press.

Jaworski, A. and Coupland, N. (1999a) 'Introduction: perspectives on discourse analysis' in A. Jaworski and N. Coupland (eds) *The Discourse Reader*. London: Routledge.

Jaworski, A. and Coupland, N. (1999b) (eds) *The Discourse Reader*. London: Routledge.

Jenkins, K. (1991) *Re-thinking History*. London: Routledge.

Jessop, B. (1982) *The Capitalist State: Marxist Theories and Methods*. Oxford: Martin Robertson.

Krasner, S. (1996) 'The accomplishments of international political economy' in S. Smith, K. Booth and M. Zalewski (eds) *International Theory: Positivism and Beyond*. Cambridge: Cambridge University Press.

Kuhn, T. (1970) *The Structure of Scientific Revolutions*, 2nd edn. Chicago: Chicago University Press.

Labov, W. and Fanshel, D. (1977) *Therapeutic Discourse: Psychotherapy as Conversation*. New York: Academic Press.

Lacan, J. (1977) *Écrits: A Selection*. London: Tavistock.

Laclau, E. (1977) *Politics and Ideology in Marxist Theory*. London: New Left Books.

Laclau, E. (1983) 'The impossibility of society', *Canadian Journal of Political and Social Theory*, 7(1/2): 21–4.

Laclau, E. (1989) 'Politics and the limits of modernity' in A. Ross (ed.) *Universal Abandon? The Politics of Postmodernism*. London: Routledge.

Laclau, E. (1990) *New Reflections on the Revolution of Our Time*. London: Verso.

Laclau, E. (1992) 'Universalism, particularism, and the question of identity', *October*, 61: 83–90.

Laclau, E. (1993) Discourse, in R. E. Goodin and P. Pettit (eds), *A Companion to Contemporary Political Philosophy*. Oxford: Blackwell.

Laclau, E. (ed.) (1994) *The Making of Political Identities*. London: Verso.

Laclau, E. (1995) 'Subject of politics, politics of the subject', *Differences*, 7(1): 145–64.

Laclau, E. (1996a) *Emancipation(s)*. London: Verso.

Laclau, E. (1996b) The death and resurrection of the theory of ideology, *Journal of Political Ideologies*, 1(3): 201–20.

Laclau, E. (1998) 'Paul de Man and the politics of rhetoric', *Pretexts: Studies in Writing and Culture*, 7(2): 153–70.

Laclau, E. and Mouffe, C. (1985) *Hegemony and Socialist Strategy*. London: Verso.

Laclau, E. and Mouffe, C. (1987) 'Post-Marxism without apologies', *New Left Review*, 166: 79–106.

Laclau, E. and Zac, L. (1984) 'Minding the gap: the subject of politics' in E. Laclau (ed.) *The Making of Political Identities*. London: Verso.

Landman, T. (2000) *Issues and Methods in Comparative Politics*. London: Routledge.

Larrain, J. (1979) *The Concept of Ideology*. London: Hutchinson.

Larrain, J. (1994) *Ideology and Cultural Identity: Modernity and the Third World Presence*. Cambridge: Polity Press.

Leach, E. (1974) *Lévi-Strauss*. London: Fontana.

Lévi-Strauss, C. (1968) *Structural Anthropology. Volume One*. Harmondsworth: Penguin.

Lévi-Strauss, C. (1969) *Totemism*. Harmondsworth: Penguin.

Lévi-Strauss, C. (1972) *The Savage Mind*. Oxford: Oxford University Press.

Lévi-Strauss, C. (1977) *Structural Anthropology. Volume Two*. Harmondsworth: Penguin.

Lévi-Strauss, C. (1987) *Introduction to the Writings of Marcel Mauss*, London: Routledge.

Lévi-Strauss, C. (1994) *The Raw and the Cooked*. London: Pimlico.

MacIntyre, A. (1978) *Against the Self-Images of the Age: Essays on Ideology and Philosophy*. Notre Dame, IN: University of Notre Dame Press.

Malcolm, N. (1993) *Wittgenstein: A Religious Point of View*. London: Routledge.

Mannheim, K. (1936) *Ideology and Utopia: An Introduction to the Sociology of Knowledge*. New York: Harvest.

Marx, K. (1977a) 'Preface to *A Critique of Political Economy*' in D. McLellan (ed.) *Karl Marx: Selected Writings*. Oxford: Oxford University Press.

Marx, K. (1977b) *The Eighteenth Brumaire of Louis Bonaparte* in D. McLellan (ed.) *Karl Marx: Selected Writings*. Oxford: Oxford University Press.

Marx, K. (1977c) *The Civil War In France* in D. McLellan (ed.), *Karl Marx: Selected Writings*. Oxford: Oxford University Press.

Marx, K. (1992) *Capital: A Critique of Political Economy. Volume 1*. Harmondsworth: Penguin.

Marx, K. and Engels, F. (1970) *The German Ideology*. London: Lawrence and Wishart.

Marx, K. and Engels, F. (1985) *The Communist Manifesto*. Harmondsworth: Penguin.

McAdam, D., McCarthy, J. D. and Zald, M. N. (1996) *Comparative Perspectives on Social Movements: Political Opportunities, Mobilizing Structures, and Cultural Feelings*. Cambridge: Cambridge University Press.

McClintock, A. and Nixon, R. (1986) 'No names apart: the separation of word and history in Derrida's "Le dernier mot du racisme"', *Critical Inquiry*, 13: 140–54.

McLellan, D. (1995) *Ideology*, 2nd edn. Buckingham: Open University Press.

McNay, L. (1994) *Foucault: A Critical Introduction*. Cambridge: Polity.

Miliband, R. (1969) *The State in Capitalist Society*. London: Weidenfeld and Nicolson.

Milliken, J. (1999) 'The study of discourse in international relations', *European Journal of International Relations*, 5(2): 257–86.

Mitchell, T. (1991) *Colonising Egypt*. Cambridge: Cambridge University Press.

Močnik, R. (1993) 'Ideology and fantasy' in E. A. Kaplan and M. Sprinker (eds) *The Althusserian Legacy*. London: Verso.

Morrice, D. (1996) *Philosophy, Science and Ideology in Political Thought*. London: Macmillan.

Mouffe, C. (1979) 'Hegemony and ideology in Gramsci' in C. Mouffe (ed.) *Gramsci and Political Theory*. London: Routledge.

Mouffe, C. (1989) 'Radical democracy: modern or postmodern?' in A. Ross (ed.) *Universal Abandon? The Politics of Postmodernism*. London: Routledge.

Mouffe, C. (ed.) (1992) *Dimensions of Radical Democracy: Pluralism, Citizenship, Community*. London: Verso.

Mouffe, C. (1993) *The Return of the Political*. London: Verso.

Mouffe, C. (1996) 'Deconstruction, pragmatism and the politics of democracy' in C. Mouffe (ed.) *Deconstruction and Pragmatism*. London: Routledge.

Mouffe, C. (2000) *The Democratic Paradox*. London: Verso.

Mouzelis, N. P. (1988) Marxism or post-Marxism?, *New Left Review*, 167: 107–25.

Mouzelis, N. P. (1990) *Post-Marxist Alternatives: The Construction of Social Orders*. Basingstoke: Macmillan.

Mulhall, S. (1996) *Heidegger and Being and Time*. London: Routledge.

Munslow, A. (1992) *Discourse and Culture*. London: Routledge.

Nairn, T. (1990) *The Enchanted Glass: Britain and Its Monarchy*. London: Picador.

Nietzsche, F. (1968) *The Will to Power*. New York: Vintage.

Norris, C. (1993) *The Truth about Postmodernism*. Oxford: Blackwell.

Norval, A. J. (1990) 'Letter to Ernesto' in E. Laclau, *New Reflections on the Revolution of Our Time*. London: Verso.

Norval, A. J. (1994) 'Social ambiguity and the crisis of apartheid' in E. Laclau (ed.) *The Making of Political Identities*. London: Verso.

Norval, A. J. (1996) *Deconstructing Apartheid Discourse*. London: Verso.

Norval, A. J. (2000) 'Future trajectories of research in discourse theory: political frontiers, myths, and imaginaries' in D. Howarth, A. J. Norval and Y. Stavrakakis (eds) *Discourse Theory and Political Analysis*. Manchester: Manchester University Press.

Osborne, P. (1991) 'Radicalism without limit' in P. Osborne (ed.) *Socialism and the Limits of Liberalism*. London: Verso.

Owen, D. (1994) *Maturity and Modernity: Nietzsche, Weber, Foucault and the Ambivalence of Reason*. London: Routledge.

Parker, I. (1992) *Discourse Dynamics: Critical Analysis for Social and Individual Psychology*. London: Routledge.

Pêcheux, M. (1982) *Language, Semantics and Ideology*. London: Macmillan.

Pêcheux, M., Henry, P., Poitou, J.-P. and Haroche, C. (1978) 'Are the masses an inanimate object?' in D. Sankoff (ed.) *Linguistic Variation*. New York: Academic Press.

Piaget, J. (1971) *Structuralism*. London: Routledge & Kegan Paul.

Plamenatz, J. (1970) *Ideology*. London: Macmillan.

Poole, R. (1969) 'Introduction' in C. Lévi-Strauss, *Totemism*. Harmondsworth: Penguin.

Popper, K. (1959) *The Logic of Scientific Discovery*, 2nd edn. London: Hutchinson.

Potter, J. and Wetherell, M. (1987) *Discourse and Social Psychology*. London: Sage.

Poulantzas, N. (1973) *Political Power and Social Classes*. London: New Left Books.

Poulantzas, N. (1978) *State, Power, Socialism*. London: New Left Books.

Quine, W. V. O. (1980) *From a Logical Point of View*. Cambridge, MA: Harvard University Press.

Rabinow, P. and Sullivan, W. M. (1979) *Interpretive Social Science: A Reader*. Berkeley: University of California Press.

Ricoeur, P. (1970) *Freud and Philosophy: An Essay on Interpretation*. New Haven, CT: Yale University Press.

Ricoeur, P. (1971) 'The model of the text: meaningful action considered as a text', *Social Research*, 38(3): 529–62.

Ricoeur, P. (1976) *Interpretation Theory: Discourse and the Surplus of Meaning*. Fort Worth: Texas Christian University Press.

Rorty, R. (1980) *Philosophy and the Mirror of Nature*. Oxford: Basil Blackwell.

Rorty, R. (ed.) (1992a) *The Linguistic Turn: Essays in Philosophic Method*. Chicago: University of Chicago Press.

Rorty, R. (1992b) *Consequences of Pragmatism*. Brighton: Harvester Press.

Rustin, M. (1988) 'Absolute voluntarism: critique of a post-Marxist concept of hegemony', *New German Critique*, 43: 146–73.

Ryan, A. (1970) *The Philosophy of the Social Science*. London: Macmillan.

Said, E. (1975) *Beginnings: Intention and Method*. New York: Basic.

Said, E. (1978) 'The problem of textuality: two exemplary critiques', *Critical Inquiry*, 4(4): 673–714.

Said, E. (1993) *Culture and Imperialism*. London: Chatto and Windus.

Said, E. (1995). *Orientalism*, 2nd edn. Harmondsworth: Penguin.

Saussure, F. de (1974) *Course in General Linguistics*. London: Fontana.

Saussure, F. de (1983) *Course in General Linguistics*. London: Duckworth.

Schatzki, T. R. (1996) *Social Practices: A Wittgensteinian Approach to Human Activity and the Social*. Cambridge: Cambridge University Press.

Schegloff, E. and Sacks, H. (1973) 'Opening up closings', *Semiotica*, 8: 289–327.

Scott, J. C. (1985) *Weapons of the Weak: Everyday Forms of Peasant Resistance*. New Haven, CT: Yale University Press.

Searle, J. (1969) *Speech Acts: An Essay in the Philosophy of Language*. Cambridge: Cambridge University Press.

Shapiro, M. (1981) *Language and Political Understanding*. New Haven, CT: Yale University Press.

Sim, S. (1998) 'Spectres and nostalgia: *post*-Marxism/post-*Marxism*' in S. Sim (ed.) *Post-Marxism: A Reader*. Edinburgh: Edinburgh University Press.

Skinner, Q. (1969) Meaning and understanding in the history of ideas, *History and Theory*, 8: 3–53.

Skocpol, T. (1979) *States and Social Revolutions: A Comparative Analysis of France, Russia and China*. Cambridge: Cambridge University Press.

Smith, A. M. (1994a) *New Right Discourse on Race and Sexuality: Britain 1968–1990*. Cambridge: Cambridge University Press.

Smith, A. M. (1994b) 'Rastafari as resistance and the ambiguities of essentialism in the "new social movements" ' in E. Laclau (ed.) *The Making of Political Identities*. London: Verso.

Smith, A. M. (1998) *Laclau and Mouffe: The Radical Democratic Imaginary*. London: Routledge.

Smith, S. (1995) 'The self-images of a discipline' in K. Booth and S. Smith (eds) *International Relations Theory Today*. Cambridge: Polity Press.

Snow, D. A. and Benford, R. D. (1988) 'Ideology, frame resonance, and participant mobilization' in B. Klandermans, H. Kriesi and S. Tarrow (eds) *From Structure to Action: Social Movement Participation across Cultures*. Greenwich, CT: JAI Press.

Sperber, D. (1979) 'Claude Lévi-Strauss' in J. Sturrock (ed.) *Structuralism and Since: From Lévi-Strauss to Derrida*. Oxford: Oxford University Press.

Staten, H. (1984) *Wittgenstein and Derrida*. Lincoln: University of Nebraska Press.

Stavrakakis, Y. (1999) *Lacan and the Political*. London: Routledge.

Stones, R. (1996) *Sociological Reasoning: Towards a Past-Modern Sociology*. London: Macmillan.

Sturrock, J. (1979) 'Introduction' in J. Sturrock (ed.) *Structuralism and Since: From Lévi-Strauss to Derrida*. Oxford: Oxford University Press.

Taylor, C. (1971) 'Interpretation and the sciences of man', *Review of Metaphysics*, 25(1): 3–51.

Taylor, C. (1985) *Philosophy and the Human Sciences, Philosophical Papers 2*. Cambridge: Cambridge University Press.

Taylor, C. (1992) 'To follow a rule' in M. Hjort (ed.) *Rules and Conventions: Literature, Philosophy, Social Theory*. Baltimore: Johns Hopkins University Press.

Texier, J. (1979) 'Gramsci, theoretician of the superstructures' in C. Mouffe (ed.) *Gramsci and Marxist Theory*. London: Routledge & Kegan Paul.

Torfing, J. (1998) *Politics, Regulation and the Modern Welfare State.* London: Macmillan.

Torfing, J. (1999) *New Theories of Discourse: Laclau, Mouffe and Žižek.* Oxford: Blackwell.

Trask, R. L. (1999) *Key Concepts in Language and Linguistics.* London: Routledge.

Tully, J. (1995) *Strange Multiplicity: Constitutionalism in an Age of Diversity.* Cambridge: Cambridge University Press.

Tully, J. (1999) 'To think and act differently: Foucault's four reciprocal objections to Habermas' theory' in S. Ashenden and D. Owen (eds) *Foucault contra Habermas: Recasting the Dialogue between Genealogy and Critical Theory.* London: Sage.

van Dijk, T. (1985) *Handbook of Discourse Analysis*, 4 vols. London: Academic Press.

van Dijk, T. (1997a) *Discourse as Social Interaction.* London: Sage.

van Dijk, T. (1997b) *Discourse as Structure and Process.* London: Sage.

Veyne, P. (1997) 'Foucault revolutionizes history' in A. I. Davidson (ed.) *Foucault and His Interlocutors.* Chicago: University of Chicago Press.

Visker, R. (1992) 'Habermas on Heidegger and Foucault: meaning and validity in the *Philosophical Discourse of Modernity*', *Radical Philosophy*, 61: 15–22.

Visker, R. (1993) 'Raw being and violent discourse: Foucault, Merleau-Ponty and the (dis)order of things' in P. Burke and J. van der Veken (eds) *Merleau-Ponty in Contemporary Perspective.* Dordrecht: Kluwer Academic Publishers.

Visker, R. (1995) *Michel Foucault.* London: Verso.

Weber, M. (1978) *Economy and Society: An Outline of Interpretive Sociology. Volume One.* Berkeley: University of California Press.

White, H. (1978) *Tropics of Discourse.* Baltimore, MD: Johns Hopkins University Press.

White, H. (1987) *The Content of the Form: Narrative Discourse and Historical Representation.* Baltimore, MD: Johns Hopkins University Press.

Williams, G. (1999) *French Discourse Analysis: The Method of Poststructuralism.* London: Routledge.

Williams, P. and Chrisman, L. (eds) (1993) *Colonial Discourse and Postcolonial Theory: A Reader.* Hemel Hempstead: Harvester Wheatsheaf.

Willing, C. (1999) *Applied Discourse Analysis.* Buckingham: Open University Press.

Winch, P. (1964) 'Understanding a primitive society', *American Philosophical Quarterly*, 1: 307–24.

Winch, P. (1990) *The Idea of a Social Science and Its Relation to Philosophy*, 2nd edn. London: Routledge.

Wittgenstein, L. (1953) *Philosophical Investigations.* Oxford: Basil Blackwell.

Wittgenstein, L. (1972) *Tractatus Logico-philosophicus*. London: Routledge & Kegan Paul.

Wittgenstein, L. (1977) *Remarks on Colour*. Oxford: Basil Blackwell.

Wodak, R. (1996) *Disorders of Discourse*. London: Longman.

Wolf, E. C. (1971) *Peasant Wars of the Twentieth Century*. London: Faber and Faber.

Wolpe, H. (1988) *Race, Class and the Apartheid State*. London: James Curry.

Wood, A. (1981) *Karl Marx*. London: Routledge & Kegan Paul.

Wood, E. (1998) *The Retreat from Class: A New 'True' Socialism*. London: Verso.

Woodiwiss, A. (1990) *Social Theory after Postmodernism*. London: Pluto.

Young, R. (1990) *White Mythologies: Writing History and the West*. London: Routledge.

Zerilli, L. M. (1998) 'This universalism which is not one', *Diacritics*, 28(2): 3–20.

Žižek, S. (1989) *The Sublime Object of Ideology*. London: Verso.

Žižek, S. (1990) 'Beyond discourse-analysis' in E. Laclau, *New Reflections on the Revolution of Our Time*. London: Verso.

Žižek, S. (ed.) (1994) *Mapping Ideology*. London: Verso.

Žižek, S. (1999) *The Ticklish Subject*. London: Verso.

Index

Index 161

Hall, S., 9, 87
Harris, R., 19, 22
Hegel, G. W. F., 80, 90, 92
hegemony, 6, 84, 89–90, 98, 100,
    109–11, 131
  projects, 102, 116, 118, 123–4, 136
Heidegger, M., 9–10, 14, 47, 112,
    114, 116, 133
hermeneutics, 4–5, 7, 10–11, 62,
    126–30
hermeneutics of recovery/retrieval,
    129
hermeneutics of suspicion, 129
historical bloc, 38, 91, 109
Hjelmslev, L., 10, 32
Homo economicus, 9
Howarth, D., 10, 41, 106, 136, 138
human beings
  external object, image or
    ideology, 95
  transformed into subjects, 79–80
human sciences, ignoble archives,
    77
human spirit, teleological
    development, 27
human subject, ideological effect,
    94
Husserl, E., 40, 50, 54, 80

idealism, 65, 92
identification, 84, 98, 109, 121
identities
  antagonisms and, 136
  black and white racism, 106
  blockage or failure of, 105–6
  differential and relational, 41
  discourses of, 114
  hegemony and, 124
  linguistic, 22
  play of differences, 40
  political, 6, 136
  relational, 102, 104
  social agents and, 105
  subjects and, 33, 94
ideology

Althusser and, 92–3, 96, 100
bourgeois, 96
false consciousness and, 87, 92
feudal society and church, 93–4
Foucault's concept of, 79
Gramsci and, 88–9
integral part of all societies, 88,
    98
Laclau and, 122–3
lived relation between social
    subjects, 93
Marxist conception, 85, 97–8,
    100, 101, 126
Mouffe and, 122
negative, 87
reproduction of society and, 92,
    97–8
science and, 59–60, 93, 100
total closure by political
    projects, 122
imaginaries, 111, 136
infinite responsibility to the Other,
    123
Inkatha Movement, 106
institutions, sedimented discourses,
    120
integral state, political rule and, 91
intellectual
  role as independent critical
    consciousness, 70
  Said and specific, 71
interpellation, 94–8, 106–8
invention of the Orient, 68
Italian Fascism, 117
iterability, 41–3

Jakobson, R., 10, 32
Jaworski, A., 2, 7
Jessop, B., 112, 119–20
judgements, frameworks and,
    114–15

Kant, I., 54, 80
Keynesian welfare state,
    dislocation of, 132